The Answer Is
Baseball

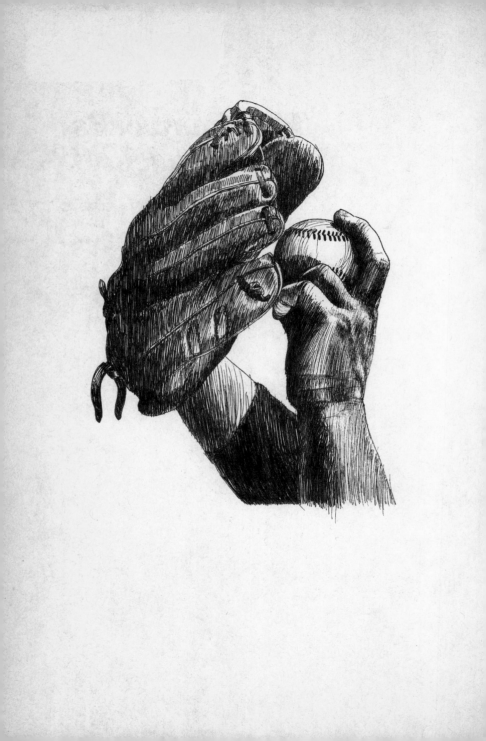

The Answer Is Baseball

A Book of Questions That Illuminate the Great Game

Luke Salisbury

Illustrations by Robert Paul Scudellari

Vintage Books
A Division of Random House, Inc.
New York

FIRST VINTAGE BOOKS EDITION, APRIL 1990

Copyright © 1989 by Luke Salisbury

Illustrations copyright © 1989 by Random House, Inc.

All rights reserved under International and Pan-American
Copyright Conventions. Published in the United States by
Vintage Books, a division of Random House, Inc., New York,
and simultaneously in Canada by Random House of
Canada Limited, Toronto. Originally published, in
hardcover, by Times Books, a division of Random House, Inc.,
New York, in 1989.

Library of Congress Cataloging-in-Publication of Data.
Salisbury, Luke, 1947–
The answer is baseball: a book of questions that illuminate
the great game/Luke Salisbury; illustrations by
Robert Paul Scudellari.
p.   cm.
Reprint. Originally published: New York: Times Books, c1989.
ISBN 0-679-72642-X
1. Baseball—Miscellanea.   I. Title.
GV867.3.S25   1990   89-40558
796.357—dc20   CIP

Book design by Cathryn S. Aison

Manufactured in the United States of America
10 9 8 7 6 5 4 3 2 1

To Barbara and Ace

Question:

What meanest thou by this word *Sacrament?*

Answer:

I mean an outward and visible sign of an inward
and spiritual grace given unto us. . . .

Question:

How many parts are there in a Sacrament?

Answer:

Two; the outward visible sign, and the inward
spiritual grace.

> —A Catechism
> *The Book of Common Prayer*
> According to the Use of
> the Protestant Episcopal Church
> in the United States of America

Contents

x

The Eternal Present

THERE are two kinds of trivia questions: those that are worth answering, and those that are not. Some questions are a door to the past and open the imagination. Others are trivial and warrant a resounding "Who cares?" Good questions can reveal changes in the way the game was played, and cause us to reevaluate reputations, compare eras, or define the parameters of greatness. Others are trivial.

"Who led the American League second basemen in doubles in 1902?" is not an interesting question. It doesn't require thinking or provide insight, and it can simply be looked up in Macmillan's *Baseball Encyclopedia*. This is information retrieval, and machines do it better than humans.

The next level of trivia comprises oddity questions. Who hit a home run in his first and last at-bats, and hit only two home runs in his career? The answer is John Miller, who inaugurated his career for the Yankees with a homer in '66, and homered again, for the Dodgers, in '69 as he bid the major leagues farewell with a .164 life average. That a player named Miller did this is not significant; that a man could have such a career is interesting.

Other questions that rise above mechanical minutiae are those that make us review the parade of men we've spent our lives watching. What two men played for the Mets in the sixties, seventies, and eighties? This is better than the John Miller question, and even a casual fan should get part of the answer: Tom Seaver. The other man isn't so easy. A fan might guess a third baseman, since the Mets tried 78 third sackers in their first 25 years, but the Met who kept returning was Mike Jorgensen, one of those players good enough to stay in the big leagues for almost three generations, but not quite good enough to start.

The best questions make us think. A good question, or better, a series of good questions—a catechism—can, like a logical argument, lead to discovery. Good questions make us seekers of baseball's truth. Consider this series:

What Triple Crown winner hit 50 home runs?

The Triple Crown is the ultimate hitting feat—it combines power with some speed (slew-feet rarely win batting titles), and RBIs require timely hitting. The Triple Crown may not be the most scientific method for determining a great season in Bill James's era of algebraic tricks and new statistics, but it's the most prestigious, which means players consciously strive for it.

The answer is not Babe Ruth. Ruth never won the Triple Crown. The Babe won a batting title, hitting .378 in 1924, and hit a league-leading 46 homers, but was second in RBIs, with 121 to Goose

Goslin's 129. This question gives us the parameters of Ruth's greatness. He won 12 homer titles and led in RBIs six times. He did not hit for average, or chose not to. Ruth never hit .400; he did hit .393, but baseball numbers are absolute. Babe Ruth did not do everything.

The answer isn't Willie Mays. Mays hit 50 homers twice, but never won the Triple Crown. In fact, Mays never led in RBIs. This tells us about the great sluggers in the National League in the fifties and sixties. It's hard to win the Triple Crown when competing against Roberto Clemente for average, Ernie Banks for homers, and Hank Aaron for all three. Aaron also never won the Triple Crown, but did win two legs of it three times. The NL was so strong that neither Mays, Aaron, Clemente, nor Frank Robinson could win the Triple Crown. Had any of them been in the American League, they would have dominated the way Robinson did in '66.

The answer is Mickey Mantle, who hit 52 homers in his Triple Crown year, 1956. This question puts Mantle's great and damaged talent in perspective. He is the only player to hit 50 home runs and win a batting title.

Has a Triple Crown winner ever led in stolen bases?

This question goes to the heart of power and speed, and the answer is yes, but not in our era. To answer this question, a fan must marshal his knowledge and attack it with common sense and a willingness to make an intelligent guess. Most fans know that home runs weren't hit in large numbers before the introduction of the "live" ball in 1920. Who was the best hitter before 1920? That's easy. Ty Cobb, and Cobb is the answer. Ty won the Triple Crown in 1909, hitting only nine homers but stealing a league-leading 76 bases. Cobb is the inverse of Ruth. He only led in home runs once but won 12 batting titles, while Ruth only led in batting once but won 12 homer crowns. This is the yin and yang of hitting.

Who won two legs of the Triple Crown the most times?

The answer demonstrates how dominating a player can be, and it's not Cobb, who did it three times. Babe Ruth won two legs of the TC seven times. No one else has done it more than three times.

Cobb's dead-ball Triple Crown leads to other questions. Who won the first Triple Crown? And how often was the TC won during the dead-ball era? Between 1876 (the founding of the National League) and 1910, the ball had a cork center, and the Triple Crown was won only four times. In 1911, a rubber-and-cork-centered ball replaced the cork cadaver, and averages went up. Between 1911 and 1919 there was only one TC winner, Heinie Zimmerman. Since 1920, the beginning of the live-ball era, there have been eleven. The history of the Triple Crown is a thumbnail sketch of the history of hitting.

The first Triple Crown was won by Paul Hines in 1878 with four homers, 50 RBIs, and a .358 average in a 60-game schedule. Hines, an excellent outfielder and early star, is worthy of note, but his Crown seems incidental. Hugh Duffy won in 1894 with a booming .438 average (highest since 1876), 18 homers, and 145 RBIs. This is a great season by any standards, but hitters had a decided advantage. The pitching mound had been moved from 50 feet to 60 feet 6 inches in '93, and pitchers hadn't adjusted.

Has the Triple Crown ever been won by someone hitting .400?

This is another way of asking just how good a season a man can have, and the answer is yes, Nap Lajoie did it with the dead ball in 1901 while hitting .422, but '01 is the first year the American League is credited with major-league status, so, as great as this year was, it needs to be taken with a grain of hindsight.

The other two .400 TC years were done by the same man: Rogers Hornsby. I don't think this feat can be overpraised. In 1922 Hornsby hit .401 with 42 homers and 152 RBIs, making him the only man to hit .400 and 40 homers. In '25, he hit .403 with 39 homers and 143 RBIs. This was in the 1920s, when averages were high, but in the two Triple Crown years, Hornsby out-hit his nearest rival by 47 and 36 points respectively.

In 1985, Ty Cobb and Pete Rose were compared because of the career-hit record. It should be pointed out that Rose never came close to winning the Triple Crown, hitting .400, or leading in stolen bases. Cobb hit .400 three times, and led in stolen

7

bases six times, in slugging eight times, and in RBIs four times. Rose was never close in any of these categories. Pete didn't have speed or power. He was an excellent player, but he doesn't deserve the company of Hornsby and Cobb.

THIS book is about trivia that isn't trivial. It is about Trivia with a capital *T,* those short questions that probe the long memory, make a fan review his knowledge, shuffle his prejudices, and think. Trivia is more than a dialogue between the present and the past, it is a dialogue in baseball's eternal present. In no sport is the present so alive with the past as baseball. Look at the mirrors that can reflect Jose Canseco. In 1988 he became the first man to hit 40 home runs and steal 40 bases in a season. There is a question that reveals the company Canseco may keep: Name the players who hit 250 homers and stole 250 bases. The answer—and remember that none of them ever hit 40 and stole 40 in a season— is Willie Mays, Bobby Bonds, Joe Morgan, Don Baylor, and Vada Pinson.

Good questions show us worlds within the world of the present. To play Trivia is to be both historian and perhaps philosopher. Trivia is the fan's Socratic method. It is a spoken covenant with complexity. Anyone who can construct a baseball catechism is more than a passive consumer.

Baseball is a body of knowledge. It has lore, history, numbers, aprocryphal stories, myths, and revelations. It is a world of its own happening in two dimensions: past and present—the field, and the imagination of the fan. The actual game can be slow; ten minutes of action is spread over two and a half hours, but the game a fan plays in his head is anything but slow. The poet Donald Hall said, "Baseball is best played in the theater of the mind." The entrance to that theater is catechism.

CATECHISM is a covenant with the complexity of the game, but complexity isn't just lying there like a bunt to be scooped up for the trouble of bending over. It has to be discovered, understood, and constructed. This requires a plan.

How are we to navigate through this phantasmagoria that started before Custer lost his scalp, marched through last summer, and is so deeply rooted in our childhood? I like the question-and-answer method. I don't like question-and-answer *books*. They gather dust on my shelves. One hunts through text that resembles a final exam—the authors seem to be paid by the question mark—and then the answers may consist only of a name, a word, or a number. This is fine for quizzing a bleachermate; but to really enjoy a good question and a good answer, one has to be able to see how the information branches out and illuminates the game's history and humors.

Is there a perfect series of questions? Is there a catechism that will bring the past and the present together with such clarity and resonance that the answers will light up the baseball sky like those flashes of lightning that showed Huck and Jim the snags and towheads in the river during storms?

There's a touch of blasphemy in looking for perfection, just as there is in falling in love, but a search ought to be an *ultimate* search. There are perils in looking for the best—in wanting the best, needing the best—and looking for The Perfect Questions (hereinafter referred to as TPQ), searching for these white whales of questions, these equivalents of Ted Williams's swing, may be like asking who wrote Shakespeare, demanding proof of the existence of God, or searching for the party or parties who were on the Grassy Knoll that day in Dallas. This quest may be proof of nothing but madness; but I say looking for questions that must be a classical blend of the sublime and ridiculous, a catechism that could stump the Sphinx or make Satan smile, that might be as luminous as the Grail and as elusive as V.,—this, gentlemen and ladies, may well be worth the trouble.

THE word *trivia* has an interesting derivation. The original meaning of the word is close to what I mean by *catechism. Trivia* comes from the Latin word *trivium,* which means a crossroads where three roads meet (*tres* meaning three, *via* road), and subsequently came to mean anything common or ordinary that could be found at the crossroads. In the Middle Ages, the *trivium* was that part of the curriculum that included grammar, rhetoric, and logic. The literal meaning of the word—"three roads"—is what I mean by *catechism:* a meeting of the past, present, and imagination.

Of all the sports, only baseball generates Trivia

worthy of the word's origin. Only baseball is the meeting place of the three roads. Have you ever heard a good football trivia question? Football is one game: winning. So is basketball. The statistics are for losers and the trivia is for nuts. The essence of these games is man-on-man competition, "beating your man," "total domination." Watching football is a different experience from watching baseball. I watch it. Football mesmerizes me, but not because the experience is a meeting of the past, present, and imagination, even though I've been watching it as long as baseball. Football doesn't make me think of records, great plays, and the way the sport was once played, or make me want to compare the men I see now to men I saw before. I know they're better now. They're bigger and faster, and the kind of actions required in football depend on size and speed. Modern conditioning and medicine make comparisons with the past ridiculous. Football's numbers are just statistics. Do Dan Marino's 48 touchdown passes in a season constitute a mark like Ruth's 60 home runs? Is Steve Largent's string of consecutive catches as exciting as DiMaggio's hitting streak? No and No.

The essence of baseball is hitting, and hitting is magic. Swatting a three-inch-diameter sphere with a piece of round wood is a God-given skill that cannot be improved by conditioning, or compensated for by teammates. Ty Cobb batting against Walter Johnson's sizzling fastball stimulates my imagination in a way that Bronko Nagurski running over 180-pound linebackers who did the forty in 5.5 seconds does not.

11

Watching football is like watching pornography. There's plenty of action, and I can't take my eyes off it, but when it's over, I wonder why the hell I spent an afternoon doing it. I like one team and dislike the other because of the kind of force they represent: finesse, raw power, head-hunting, trickery, and so on. One team usually emerges as a bully. It's not just that a team gets beaten, it gets beaten up. Football is exciting. I don't deny its power or its applicability to contemporary, violent America, but football's roads converge in a dark place.

Baseball is played by men of normal build doing something magic.

UNLIKE other sports, baseball's past is always relevant; its distant mirrors renew the present, and the present revives the past. This is not only because baseball has the longest history, but because it transcends winning with a variety of delights. Rod Carew's seven batting titles and no pennants don't make him a loser but put him in the company of Musial and Wagner, while Wilt Chamberlain's seven scoring titles and two championships make him a candidate for psychohistory and comparisons with Richard Nixon. There is only one game in basketball: winning—invulnerability under pressure. If a man doesn't win, everything else is a cover. Wilt's scoring titles are no better than feathers. In baseball, success can be subtle, and individual feats can shine despite team feebleness. Carew, unlike Chamberlain and Nixon, understood the game he played.

The sports that don't generate Trivia don't have interesting regular seasons. Football and basketball have "playoff seasons" that are the money seasons. The NBA has trivialized its regular season to the point where a major television network doesn't televise a weekly game until January. The betting habits of the American public keep this from happening to the NFL.

Almost by definition, the greatest moments in "clock sports" come at their ends. Fans remember buzzer-beating jump shots, last-second sweat, and the combat intensity of a game-deciding play. The most meaningful record of these championship-oriented, "now" sports is visual. No statistic, anecdote, or insight can explain how Bird could pass, Bill Russell block shots, Swann make those catches in the Super Bowl, or O. J. Simpson cut around linebackers. These games have visual memories. Baseball has a different sort of memory. Even while the game is played, the past and present mingle in a fan's imagination. Roger Maris spent the last two months of the 1961 season chasing Babe Ruth, and this battle excited fans more than the pennant race. When Dan Marino broke Y. A. Tittle's touchdown record in '84, there was no chase, no quest. Football is instant, violent gratification. Basketball is grace under pressure. These games have no equivalent of 61 homers, a .400 average, or a 56-game hitting streak. Baseball fans have standards.

THE baseball past is a world the establishment can't touch. They can't cheapen it. They can expand, play on plastic, add wild-card teams to the playoffs, have a DH for every position, start the World Series on Christmas Day, or play the whole season in a television studio in Japan, but the lords of baseball and television moguls can't hurt the past. They can't package it, copyright it, move it out of Brooklyn. No one can hook your memory up to cable system and charge a monthly fee. The past is ours.

I don't favor the past over the present—baseball exists symbiotically in the past *and* the present —but I certainly enjoy summoning up, through Trivia, a world without the DH, where the pennant race ended in the pennant. In 1969, baseball copied the NFL, expanded, and opted for a playoff system. The DH is nowhere near as radical a break with baseball's past and basic structure as are divisions and playoffs. League Championship Series? LCS? LCS is high-tech newspeak. "The World Series" is one of the great phrases in the American language. "The League Championship Series" has barely caught on with sportscasters. Surely God intended us to have two arms, two legs, two Testaments, and two leagues. Two leagues, playing the long season and each sending a champion to the World Series, was a grand design. In 1969, the lords of baseball decided that tradition and symmetry couldn't compete with ratings and dollars (only in baseball could one expect tradition and symmetry to be worth a damn), and the basic structure was changed.

No longer is there that ultimate moment: the regular-season, pennant-winning home run. We have LCS-winning home runs. They're exciting, but the LCS comes every year, like Labor Day. The lords have taken away those moments of absolute fury—Bobby Thompson's home run (hit in a play-off, but a playoff after two teams had played 154 games and tied); Yaz's October weekend against the Twins; the Yankees–Red Sox pennant war in '49. Chris Chambliss's home run against the Royals in '76 was fine, but there's nothing epic about winning the LCS. Like the Jerry Lewis telethon, it happens every year. There can never be another Bobby Thompson home run. There can never be another September of 1967; those Red Sox may have been one of the weakest peacetime teams to ever win a pennant, but they won the pennant, not the Eastern Division. They beat nine other teams in a 162-game race. I shouldn't complain. I watch the LCS. I'm one of those people who like the security of knowing there's a baseball game on television at the end of the day. When the last World Series game is over I feel like Persephone—six months on Olympus must be followed by six in hell—but that doesn't mean I don't lament mixing the wine with water. Those moments of supreme excitement—the once-in-a-lifetime moments, which actually come two or three times in a generation—will never come again. Nothing in sports was ever as exciting as playing the whole season to win the pennant, and nothing ever will be.

I was forced into baseball's other worlds by the strike of 1981. I'd always enjoyed the game's history and Trivia, but that summer I was like a junkie without a fix—restless, irritable, depressed. International League baseball was on ESPN, the all-sports channel, and like many other addicts, I watched, figuring that minor-league ball would serve as a substitute until the real stuff arrived. It didn't. I found the games interesting, but not satisfying. I knew the names of one or two players on some of the teams: Von Hayes was at Charleston, Cal Ripken at Rochester, Boggs at Pawtucket. (Wade led the IL in hitting, but no one in Boston paid attention. We thought he was another slow, hit-for-average white guy who would go the route of Chris Coletta and Billy Schlesinger.) These names give those IL games a luster they didn't have. It wasn't the quality of play—minor-league ball is fun, especially in person—it was the quality of the game in my mind. I didn't know enough to keep myself interested. One missing dimension was lifetime statistics. Minor-league stats are rarely totaled because numbers accumulated at one level aren't applicable to another, just as whole minor-league careers aren't applicable to one day in the major leagues. Every big-leaguer is playing a game with his career and every other big-league career. I couldn't find the worlds within the minor-league world. Joe Morgan's final doubles total, and Dave Kingman passing Stan Musial in home runs, are things that interest me. The minor-leaguers I saw on the 24-hour sports channel weren't building a statistical edifice. They were showing potential, skills, "face,"—the kind of thing professional baseball men look for. Minor-league numbers aren't any more significant than College Board scores. So what if a Columbus Clipper hit .275 instead of .255? These men were not

16

playing in the charmed, documented circle of major-league baseball that goes back to 1876, the year *Tom Sawyer* was published. Minor league numbers aren't written in the Book of Life.

For the first time since I was a child, I knew what people meant when they said baseball could be dull. It wasn't as bad as my wife complaining, "It's all the same endless game," but the likes of Dave Koza, Dallas Williams, and Russ Laribee couldn't sustain my interest. I realized that it takes years to build the knowledge to sit in front of a television set and watch an entire baseball game.

Desperate men seek desperate solutions. Something I depended on had stopped. Something I accepted as another reality, neither better nor worse than this one, but definitely separate and safe, turned out to be as evanescent as a love affair. It started, it stopped, and there wasn't a damn thing I could do about it. The Argentine writer Jorge Luis Borges said that to fall in love is to create a religion with a fallible god, and I had been worshiping at this shrine since I was ten. This wasn't 1972, when baseball shut down for a week (long enough to unbalance the schedule and let the Red Sox finish a game they couldn't make up behind the Tigers—but the Sox had their chance head-to-head in Detroit and Aparicio fell down). This was a long, backbreaking strike during the heart of the summer. Something had to be done.

I started going to the library and reading old newspaper sports sections. This is the most entertaining free pastime in the United States. In Boston, the microfilm reading room is only open during

17

business hours, so one encounters the bums, college students, hooky-players, and literate misfits that are to be found in a big-city library on a workday. You go into the old part of the Boston Public Library to a green room that looks as if it might be a good place to sit out the next war, and ask for *The New York Times* for September–October 1949; the *Boston Globe* for September–October 1967; or the *New York World* for April –May 1897; you are given reels of microfilm, in neatly labeled boxes, which fit into clumsy gray machines that project an image on the back wall of what looks like a tepee, and—*voila* —there is the past. To hell with the players and owners. I followed the Red Sox–Yankee pennant death march of 1949, relived the hair-raising September of 1967 when four clubs clawed, stumbled, and fought for the AL flag. (The latter was bittersweet; go read the papers from your youth and see if you don't feel the infinite loss Borges says a man feels when he sees a date from his past written in his own handwriting. I was twenty that summer, and 1967, in the parlance of the time, was "a trip": the possibilities of a bright new subversive world were everywhere. The rock and roll was wonderful —*Sgt. Pepper* at the beginning of the summer, the Doors and Jimi Hendrix by the end. The baseball was better).

On microfilm I followed the fortunes of an Indian (about whom more later) who appeared like a comet in the National League in 1897 and was soon out of the big leagues because of drink. I discovered the racy sports reporting of the 1890s, which could taunt as well as laud the home team. HAS YET TO WIN/

BOSTON/SUCCEEDS ONLY IN SCARING PHILLY, read one headline. There's a vividness to "Kid Nichols looked his man over and then sent one full-steam close to his head," that doesn't seem possible in our television world. I felt the surreal quality of fulfilled wishes with prose like, "Fifty-five-year-old Fenway Park erupted in one of the wildest scenes in major-league history at 4:33 P.M. today," and definitely felt a quiver of excitement reading a 1949 "Special to *The New York Times*" which said, "Then, next Saturday and Sunday, the Yanks and Red Sox will shoot it out in the Bronx."

The year 1981 was a disaster, but, as Coriolanus says, "There is a world elsewhere." This book is a journey into worlds elsewhere by way of questions. We shall look through the random, trivial, forgotten, and obscure for baseball's meaning. Gertrude Stein, on her death bed, was asked, "What's the answer?" and replied, "What's the question?" Answers reveal information; questions reveal the parameters of our minds. As Socrates and Freud demonstrated, questions can cleanse the soul. We shall play a game older than baseball. We will look for meaning.

A Question
That Isn't Trivial

What pitcher has the best lifetime record against the Yankees, with over 15 career wins against them?

This is good example of a question that isn't trivial. It has a blend of question and answer that can really only be termed sublime. The question is answerable. It can be deduced, free-associated, or conjured from a not-overly-large store of baseball knowledge. Like any candidate for the best question ever asked, when the answer is revealed, when the veil falls from the face of the goddess, you may well say, "I should have known it." The answer to a superb question must not only feel right ("Damn it, I knew that!"), but demonstrate a complexity and harmony not imagined.

This is a major-league question because the New York Yankees, love them or hate them (and hate is a rarefied form of homage), are the New York Yankees. They have been the best team. Saying the New York Yankees is like saying the United States —the name implies power, prestige, and nearly unbroken success. Has anything ever connoted the

23

majesty of baseball like the stately façade on the old upper deck? Or the size of the old center field? (With monuments in play—a man could hit a ball and have it touch bronze commemorating Lou Gehrig—history was in fair territory). Remember the sheer cavernous expanse of the place? I saw my first baseball game there on a chilly night in 1957 and was awed not only by the enormity of the place but by the vastness of the night it owned above it. Yankee Stadium was The Stadium, not a park like green Fenway, or a field like cozy Wrigley or campy Ebbets. Yankee Stadium was the edifice and turf to judge all others by. Its height and sweep mirrored New York's stature. The Yankees were equal to playing in such a place. They dominated the American League the way New York City dominates the American idea of the city and Wall Street dominates the economy. I use the past tense because Yankee Stadium was renovated in 1974 and 1975 and isn't The Stadium anymore. The outfield was reduced so that the dimensions the immortals had to contend with are more manageable for today's Yankees; the seats are light blue, and the upper-deck façade is gone. The imperial theme has been softened. The Stadium owns less of the night.

We do not live in an august age. Yankee Stadium has seats the color of a little boy's bedroom. Its grand shape has been muted with plastic, and the magnificent upper-deck façade is gone (at least it no longer looks down on the DH); but Yankee Stadium is still better than the McDonald's-like palaces where everything is plastic, including the infield. Tiger Stadium, a wonderful ballpark, was renovated without losing its original quirky charm. That asymmetrical cathedral, despite blue seats, still gives a fan the feel of baseball when men wore spikes, outfielders had to learn walls, and stadiums didn't look like gigantic contraceptive devices.

The Yankees have the best uniform. Even a Yankee-hater respects the pinstripes and that marvelous logo. The Yankee home uniform is The Uniform. Other clubs, such as the Dodgers, have good uniforms (unfortunately, the L.A. media mill has made the phrase "Dodger blue" as welcome to the American ear as "Islamic republic"), but Yankee pinstripes, like the old Yankee Stadium, are the standard. Even in the era of McStadiums and polyester, the Yankees haven't trifled with those elegant pinstripes.

The Yankees remain, in spite of their owner, the definitive team. As *The New York Times* once put it in the fifties, after the Washington Senators had defeated the Bronx Bombers: "Yesterday, the Senators beat the Yankees at their own game—baseball."

This question of who has beaten them most often is too good to answer quickly, so I will tell you who it is not. It's not Frank Lary, the "Yankee killer" and burly Tiger who beat New York consistently during the heyday of their perfection, the 1950s, when it seemed the Yankees always won unless the big Tiger from Huntsville, Alabama, was on the mound.

Might the Yankee beater, you ask, have thrived while the Yankees were weak? When were the Bombers second-rate? One mark of a good question is that it can be at least partially figured out. Good questions make one think, conjure, and cross-reference. What pitchers were good when the Yankees were bad? Can we find a path to the answer? Palmer and Tiant were good pitchers in the late sixties and early seventies, when New York was uncharacteristically bad. They are both good guesses, but there was another era when the Yankees struck fear in few hearts. Before 1920 and the live ball, the Yankees had been in only one race: 1904, when they were the New York Highlanders, and met the Boston Pilgrims on the last day of the season, trailing by a game, for a doubleheader. This was one of those epic, season-ending confrontations that make boys play hooky and fans squirm like Judgment Day. With the score tied 2–2 in the ninth, Jack Chesbro beat himself with a wild pitch. Until 1986, this was the only time Boston came in first and New York second.

A fan with a sense of history might recall the days when New York's AL franchise wandered in the wilderness, and figure that the pitcher with the best record against the New York Americans worked before 1920. The fan with that long a memory, or, better, a cultivated and well-researched memory might think of Walter Johnson. The big right-hander with the slingshot delivery and 110 shutouts (SABR researchers have proved the earlier figure of 113 wrong because Johnson was relieved in three shutouts) was the best pitcher of that and probably any era; but the fan with the artful memory also knows the Big Train pitched for a mediocre team and worked until 1927, when the Yankees were the team of teams. Answering a tough question may require more than a cultivated memory; it may require intuition (a four-syllable word for luck), and intuition suggests that Johnson is too obvious. The answer isn't Walter Johnson.

Rube Waddell is another superpitcher who worked exclusively in the dead-ball era when the Yankees weren't themselves. Waddell fanned 349 batters in 1904—which stood until Koufax, and is a testament to a great pitcher let loose in a weak league—but Connie Mack's supremely gifted left-hander isn't the answer. The wild man from Brad-ford, Pennsylvania, who used to leave the bench to chase fire engines doesn't own the best career rec-ord against the Highlanders and Yankees. Nor does Ed Walsh, the spitmaster and architectural consul-tant for Comiskey Park. (Charlie Comiskey asked for advice and he got it: 362-foot foul lines, and that was before the rubber-and-cork-centered ball!) It isn't Jack Coombs (who, in his short, happy career, had a 5–0 World Series record and set the AL sin-gle-season shutout mark), or Boston wonder boy Joe Wood (did a pitcher ever have a better year than Wood in 1912?), Chief Bender (did a pitcher ever have a better name?), Eddie Plank (no twentieth-century 300-game winner is so little remembered), or Cy Young.

The answer is Babe Ruth.

Babe Ruth's career record against the Yankees was 17–5. Frank Lary's was 28–13. Lary, of course, faced tougher Yankee teams and is the all-time Yan-kee-killer, but the Babe has the best percentage.

Not only is there a satisfying irony in this, but

the question and answer neatly illustrate an important fact of baseball history, the great power shift between the eras of dead and live ball. Babe Ruth held the home-run record in both eras. He hit 29 homers in 1919, while playing for the Red Sox, which broke all records, even the 27 hit by Ned Williamson in 1884 in Chicago's tiny Lake Front Park, where the right-field fence was 196 feet away. The 1919 ball was livelier than the pre-1910 cadaver, but in 1920 the ball was really jazzed up and the game changed. Ruth shattered his record of 29 by hitting 54, which is a quantum leap on the order of manned flight or nuclear war. That same year George Sisler set the season-hit mark with 257, the NL batting average went from .258 to .270, and the AL average went from .268 to .283. The statistic always mentioned about 1920, as well it should be, is that Ruth not only out-homered every other *man* in the league, but every other *club*.

That year, 1920, is the beginning of what may look like the start of modern baseball to future historians. It's interesting to note that this coincides so precisely with the shift in sensibility we call "modern." The First World War dynamited the Victorian world out of existence just as Babe Ruth's slugging blasted away baseball's old regime of base hits and stolen bases. The "inside" game of John McGraw, with its squeezes, sacrifices, and low-run games, looked like the horse and buggy compared to Ruth's Deusenberg slugging. It was the beginning of that most American decade, the wet and roaring twenties, when, despite the pronouncements of Calvin Coolidge, America decided the business of

America was having a good time and hitting home runs.

Ruth, colossus that he is, has one foot in the "inside" baseball of the teens (he was the best left-hander in baseball when pitching and defense were supreme, and was 6–2 in ten starts against Walter Johnson) and the other, as slugger supreme, in the new world of the live ball, high batting averages, and the home run. Ruth is the pivotal figure in the game's change from its patient, nineteenth-century agrarian symmetry to the simplified and electrifying sluggers' bull market of the twenties. In no decade did the style of the game change and mirror the style of the times so closely. As America became faster-paced and more urban and pleasure-conscious (F. Scott Fitzgerald said, "The buildings were higher, the morals were looser and the liquor cheaper"), along came the live ball, Hollywood, and Babe Ruth.

No one will ever have statistics like the Babe. His back-to-back slugging percentages of .847 and .846 in 1920 and 1921 are enough to boggle anyone's mind (Roger Maris didn't challenge that record; Maris slugged .620 when he hit 61 homers), and Ruth holds what is arguably the most important modern single-season record: runs scored. What is the essence of baseball if it isn't scoring runs? Ruth scored 177 runs in 1923. It's interesting that Ruth, not Cobb, who got more hits and was a far better baserunner, scored the most runs. (The trick is walks. Here's a question: In how many seasons did Ty Cobb walk over a hundred times? Only one, so there is something other than hit home runs that

Cobb didn't do.) The next closest was Gehrig, with 167 in '36. The last man to score 150 was Ted Williams in '49. Ricky Henderson scored 146 in '85, and will probably be the next to score 150. No one will ever convince me there's a more impressive record than runs scored in a season, but there's more to Babe Ruth than all his numbers.

Babe Ruth was the first superstar, a term that reflects the modern way of merchandising greatness. After the twenties, both the selling and the perception of stars, be they sports, literary, or political figures, changed. The radio, the moving picture, the newsreel, and television changed the intensity of celebrity. A superstar, as opposed to the heroes of print, drawing, and word of mouth, is as recognizable as the President of the United States. In sports, he is synonymous with his game; and in sports, as in movies and even in politics, he brings in people who aren't fans. The public comes to see a man who is supposed to be better than best.

Ruth's times were right to promote a hero. The twenties were a self-proclaimed "golden age of sport." One of my favorite discoveries, after having been a rather unthinking devotee of the twenties mystique, was learning that New York promoter Tex Rickard used to slip reporters hundred-dollar bills to inform their readers that they were living in a "golden age." The twenties were certainly a golden age for promoting athletes. Babe Ruth, Red Grange, Bill Tilden, and Bobby Jones are far better remembered than the stars who came before them. Ruth was better than Cobb—Cobb merely perfected the "inside" game, but Ruth established a new order. Red Grange, however, wasn't as good as Jim Thorpe, who may have been the greatest college football player of all time, but there are no movies of Thorpe at Carlisle College, only stories that, as the years go by, begin to sound like tall tales. I don't even know who the best tennis player and best golfer were before the twenties, which proves my point.

The first baseball radio broadcasts started early in the decade, and America's romance with immediacy began. Action photography in newspapers started around 1910 and was commonplace by the Twenties. There's nothing like a photo, rather than an artist's conception, to make something seem real. And, of course, there were newsreels. I don't think the effect of the moving picture can be overestimated. Think of the difference in our appreciation of Cobb and Ruth. We can see Ruth in those old jerky, grainy, silent, black and white movies, hitting home runs, mincing around the bases, and waving. We see a silent Yankee Stadium rise in unison with that mighty swing and muscular follow-through that put the fear of God in three generations of pitchers. Cobb we see in action only in our minds. Baseball may play best in that theater, but reputations don't. People remember pictures.

The fact that Ruth could be seen all over America on film, rather than only in ballparks, greatly enhanced his reputation while he played. I think the fact that those movies were silent gave him an even more dramatic quality. Without sound, the illusion of reality was not complete, and the figure on the screen was somewhere between legend and dream.

Ruth really was the first baseball player whose face was as recognizable as that of the President of the United States, and it doesn't matter whether he actually said, when told he made more money than the President, "I had a better year than he did." His teammate Joe Dugan said, "All the lies about him are true," which is most high praise. The twenties may have been an era of electronic huckstering and a greased-palm "golden age," but Babe Ruth was Babe Ruth. No one has numbers close to his.

Ruth's lifetime average was .342. No one else who hit 600 homers has a lifetime average higher than .305. Only two men with 500 homers have lifetime averages over .320. When the Babe retired in 1935, only two other men had hit 300 homers. No one who retired in the thirties got to 500. (Gehrig would have, but fate cut him short.) Only two men retiring in the forties got 500 homers. No one who retired in the fifties had 500; and finally, three decades after a corpulent Babe Ruth called it quits with the Boston Braves (back in Boston at last—the first time he left was tragedy, the second farce); three decades later, great sluggers like Williams and Mantle, and good ones like Banks and Mathews, had reached 500; and by the seventies the doors of that temple had been all but blasted off by the likes of Aaron, Mays, Frank Robinson, Killebrew, McCovey —but all these men played their entire careers with the live ball, none of them pitched, and only Aaron caught the Sultan of Swat. Ruth is still ahead of our time.

It's fitting that the man who has the best career mark against the Yankees should be the greatest Yankee. This enhances both Ruth and the Yankees. Their greatest player was their silver bullet—or wooden stake, if you feel about them the way I do. This question and answer fit together like lines of poetry. There is an inevitability here that is stunning. This is fearful symmetry.

The Best
Single-Season Question

SINGLE-SEASON feats are a good place to look for questions. The season is the basic unit of baseball, not the career and not the game. Everything is predicated on winning the pennant and the World Series, and these are determined each year and only once. Baseball is not a single-elimination sport; one game can't decide much. A championship game doesn't make sense. Too many fluky things can happen in just one game ("Yesterday, the Senators beat the Yankees at their own game. . . .") Any kind of championship must be the result of season or series. The three-out-of-five LCS format, mercifully dumped after 1984, was something borrowed from basketball. A baseball season is like a life—long, different at the end from what it was at the beginning, full of ups and downs, slumps and hot streaks, finally comes to a conclusion, is judged, and finds the sleep of winter.

What happens in a season is more important than anything that can happen in a career. Henry Aaron found this out when he broke Babe Ruth's hallowed 714-career-home-run mark. Aaron was pilloried for not having been the slugger Ruth was, for having batted thousands more times to hit his homers, for never having hit 50 in a season (the Babe did it four times), and because he was black. To paraphrase H. L. Mencken, no one ever lost money underestimating the racism of the American public. Aaron was justified in complaining that the comparisons to Ruth's home-run frequency weren't fair, or were beside the point: a record is a record, and what matters is that it's been bettered. He was certainly right to object to the racial slurs, and handled them in the manly, stoic way he'd always dealt with that trash, going back to his days with Jacksonville in the South Atlantic League. Where one feels compelled to disagree with even so eminent a gentleman as Henry Aaron is his claim that once a black man broke Ruth's career home-run record, a white record, Joe DiMaggio's 56-game hitting streak, became the great record. The great record is still a home-run record, Roger Maris's single-season mark of 61.

Maris's pursuit of that record produced the most controversy and most nonsense in baseball's history. Why should a man pursuing something so special, something a fan would wait a lifetime to see, create so much havoc? This is an interesting question. If we can answer it, we may learn something about more than baseball.

Both Maris's and Aaron's pursuit of Ruth produced scorn. The reasons why may go beyond Trivia. Perhaps we should have a category called meta-questions, or mega-questions, or maybe just plain damn good questions. Anyway, an inquiry into why Babe Ruth's home-run records, single-season and career, were so important to fans and the baseball establishment is a mega-quest.

MARIS ran afoul of everyone in 1961. The American League's expansion brought in two new clubs, created a longer schedule, and added one formerly minor-league park: Wrigley Field in Los Angeles, where the Pacific Coast League Los Angeles Angels had played, and where the AL Angels played until moving briefly to Chavez Ravine. It's one of those oddities that prove truth is at least more ironic, if not stranger, than fiction, that this first year of the expanded schedule was the first year Babe Ruth's home-run record had been challenged since Hank Greenberg's heroic try in '38. As soon as it became apparent that Mickey Mantle and Roger Maris were actually chasing the Babe, the great debate began. What constituted a season? Arthur Daley of the *Times* said a season was a season regardless of the number of games, but many self-proclaimed purists came forward, saying a season was 154 games, the Ruth season. Everyone had an opinion. The issue attracted more attention in the *Times* than the later controversy surrounding President Kennedy's assassination. The Commissioner of Baseball responded, as someone at the top of bureaucracy always will, with a spineless compromise: the asterisk. Ford Frick decreed that if the record were broken, the new mark would bear an asterisk accompanied by a disclaimer pointing out that post-1960 home runs were hit in a 162-game schedule.

There has never been anything like the asterisk—or, as it turned out, the threat of the asterisk. No record has ever been so jealously guarded. Did anyone suggest that Pete Rose, or Aaron, for that matter, an asterisk placed beside their lifetime hit and homer totals? Since 1962 the National League has played the 162-game schedule. That means Rose got an extra eight games every year of his career. Over a twenty-year span, that's 160 games, or another entire season. No one did, and I have to return to my original point: season records are of a higher magnitude than career records. A career is longevity, a season is genius under fire. A career record is like having a good character—it's nice, it helps you live longer. A single-season record is like doing well in battle.

What happened in Roger Maris's last at-bat in game 154 in 1961?

Ford Frick set the stage for Maris's agony. He announced in July that the record would have to be tied or broken in the Ruth season or carry the asterisk. Frick was a former newspaperman and a drinking buddy of Ruth's. (Can you think of anyone other than Shakespeare that you'd rather tell people was your drinking buddy? The Babe could find, make, or simply *will* action. Jack Kerouac once said, "Not even the biggest fighter, the biggest drunk, or the biggest lover can ever find the center of Saturday night in America." Kerouac never met the Babe.) Frick was also a former friend and 1961 friend of Claire Ruth, the aging, plump keeper of the Babe's domestic flame. For Claire and Frick,

Babe was the bad kid turned good father: Babe, the king of Saturday night, found happiness with Claire and the girls on the davenport; their Babe never carried a lady of the night on each shoulder while leading a Detroit judge to the second floor of a whorehouse. Frick comforted Claire and kept faith with Saturday night by proclaiming the asterisk.

For all the sound and fury, all the ludicrously unfair comparisons of Maris to Ruth, all the flapdoodle about the eight extra games, and the asterisk, there is no asterisk in the Macmillan *Baseball Encyclopedia*—either in my second printing of the first edition of 1969, or the one I bought ten years later. It turned out that no one gave a damn about the asterisk except poor Roger Maris, who lived with it until the end of his life. Maris is remembered not for breaking an unbreakable record, but for breaking a record that baseball officially refused to believe he broke. This brings us directly to the mega-question: Why was Maris treading on the sacred? Why is Babe Ruth's 60 the most important number in American sports?

This may be the American Sphinx. If we can answer this question, we may find the center of Saturday night. Part of the answer is Ruth's insatiable infantile personality—he couldn't eat enough hot dogs, screw enough whores, talk to enough kids, or hit enough home runs. He did everything big, and didn't disappoint in the clutch. The Babe was an adolescent writ large, and seems to have been sustained by a fundamental innocence that everyone realized wasn't phony. Roger Maris wasn't a happy infant. In the middle of the '61 season, the year of

41

cognitive dissonance, a New York writer wrote that Roger wasn't "Ruthian." This lead to an onslaught on Maris: he was moody, he was irritable, he wasn't a good ole beaver-shooting golden boy like Mickey Mantle or a rebellious hick like Elvis. Maris was introverted. He was a ballplayer, not a media superstar. How dare a mere ballplayer hit 60 home runs?

No one felt that way when Pete Rose eclipsed Cobb's 4,191 hits. No one decried Rose for being un-Cobbian. Pete can thank Cobb's personality. Ty Cobb was unique. I suspect there's only one a century like that—in either baseball or fiction. Ahab in the nineteenth, Ty Cobb in the twentieth. Grantland Rice said Cobb was possessed by the Furies, and for once the dapper Hercules of hyperbole couldn't be accused of overstating his case. Had Cobb been alive to see Rose challenge his record, he might have shot him.

Pete Rose has been to the media in the 1980s what Babe Ruth was to the fan in the twenties and thirties. Pete was media-perfect. The media couldn't have created a better man in its own image. As Pete approached Cobb's record, he never tired of giving interviews, talking about himself, selling himself, pushing his "Ty Breaker" T-shirts, or hawking his Ty-chasing diary. Pete never tires of center stage. He never tires of the media. William Carlos Williams said the pure products of America go crazy, but baseball seems to have its own dispensations.

One suspects that Pete might go crazy if he didn't have television cameras and microphones to record his every comment on what's left of his life in baseball. Pete's play never got him to the top. Remember, Bill James said Pete Rose was never the best player on the Cincinnati Reds, let alone the best player in baseball. It's our love of numbers, our love of the statistical game, along with Pete's obsession with publicity, that has made this phenomenon. There is no comparison between Pete Rose and Ty Cobb as ballplayers. Until Babe Ruth swaggered onstage people thought Ty Cobb was *the greatest ballplayer who ever lived*. Period. The greatest—not the man with the most hits or the longest batting streak in National League history, or the guy most remembered for a particular head-first slide seen on television. Pete Rose was no Ty Cobb, but like Ruth, he gave us what we wanted.

Players like Cobb, Maris, and Ted Williams made themselves by baseball greatness. Pete Rose half-made himself with his baseball ability. We made the rest. We need stars who don't self-destruct under celebrity. We worship celebrity, but relish its time on the cross. We put our stars through hell because celebrity is wanted so desperately by so many we insist that it must be white hot, awful, a blaze that consumes.

We need celebrities and revere the ones who never slip. We respect the ones who don't get bored, and who never, ever, act like they can live without it. Maris didn't like celebrity. He was a ballplayer, not a mythomaniac like Elvis, Pete, or even Mickey Mantle, who could good-ole-boy it into the white center of the fifties. Maris didn't fit the central myth of our popular culture: grace under publicity, that lack of private self the great ones seem to have.

America likes a mask that doesn't slip. America likes a mask with nothing behind it but a mask. Nothing behind it but Pete Rose or Ronald Reagan. The price of wearing a mask is high. Hemingway created a style and a character called Ernest Hemingway. Gary Cooper played that character in the movies, but who could play it in life? Not the man who blew his brains out in Ketchum.

But why is Babe Ruth sacred? Why the overgrown reform school boy blessed with athletic genius and an uncomplicated but savvy mind? Is this what America thinks of itself? Is this what we really want to be? The greatest player of a boys' game, the most boyish player of a boy's game? The great hitter, the sexual pilgrim, the great comforter of children—the man whose inside and outside were indistinguishable? Is this the man we would be? Home runs, chorus girls, fame without contradiction, no existential glances at the abyss, no violence waiting to happen? Do we love him because he wasn't a killer like Cobb or a driven artist like Ted Williams—or, at the end, an empty actor like Hemingway, or a drunk/addict staggering under the weight of success that can't happen again (fill in your favorite dying god: Elvis, F. Scott Fitzgerald, Kerouac, etc.).

How did Roger Maris get to the sacred turf of Yankee Stadium to chase the sacred record? This is a very good question, and the answer is considerably more complicated than just looking up Yankee transactions for 1959 in Joe Reichler's *Baseball Trade Register*. Most fans remember that Maris, and what seemed like half the Yankee squad, came from

Kansas City, but many don't remember that Maris started with Cleveland in '57. In fact, all three out-fielders on that Indian team were Yankees: one at the beginning of his career, one in the middle, and one at the end. Maris is the man who spent his middle years in New York. He was flanked by Gene Woodling and the most famous Indian of the late fifties, a man admirably suited to the hot-shot, greaser, ethnic-slugger image of the time: Rocky Colavito. Woodling played for the Yankees during their run of five straight World Championships, and platooned with men like Jackie Jensen, Johnny Lindell, Cliff Mapes, and Bob Cerv. Colavito played only 39 games for the Yankees, at the end of the 1968 season, and might be forgotten except for a memorable 2⅔-inning pitching stint against the Tigers, whom Colavito beat, just before they went on to be World Champions. I heard the last two innings on a pretzel vendor's radio in Washington Square Park. I'd just come back from Europe and was flat broke. Everyone has been young and broke in New York City, but not everyone finds something as diverting as listening to Rocky Colavito pitch.

How did Roger's seemingly inevitable journey to New York begin? Cleveland sent him to Kansas City with Dick Tomanek (remember him?—right-hand pitcher who looked good on a baseball card because his name looked like "tomahawk") and Preston Ward, a classic 1950s big-white-guy first baseman, for Vic Power and Woody Held, who both came out of the super-stocked Yankee farm system. Once Maris was in Kansas City, it was a fore-gone conclusion he would be a Yankee. In retrospect, it seems that fate brought him to New York. Where else could a man rendezvous with 60 home runs? Imagine the sacrilege of a man in a city other than New York challenging the Babe. Even an asterisk couldn't subdue that blasphemy.

But let's be careful about fate. Fate didn't bring Babe Ruth to New York—money did. Who did the Yankees trade for Roger Maris? Given what Maris did in New York, this is an important question. Trade questions are fun because they provide an idea of what a general manager thought a man was once worth. They are also fun when hindsight shows how one team got snookered. New York–Kansas City 1950s trade questions, however, are not so amusing. New York lost the pennant in '59, and turned, as it did 16 times between 1955 and 1960, to the Kansas City Athletics. This time the A's obliged by sending Roger Maris, Kent Hadley (a big, left-handed first baseman with a nice swing; Hadley looked like a Yankee), and Joe DeMastri (good field, absolutely no-hit backup shortstop), for Marv Throneberry (there's a nice piece of trivia— did you know that the man who broke Babe Ruth's home-run record was once traded for Marv Throneberry?), Norm Siebern, Don Larsen, and Hank Bauer. What a typical Yankee deal! They gave up a good prospect in Siebern (his trouble in the '58 Series in the late-October left-field sun-pit doomed him), an over-the-hill Hank Bauer (longest World Series hitting streak—17 games—that one may stand for a while), and Don Larsen, who promptly went 1–10 for KC.

Maris responded by leading the AL in RBIs and

winning the MVP award for 1960. People forget that Maris won two MVPs. He wasn't a nobody in 1961. Furthermore, Maris was built for Yankee Stadium. He was a left-hand pull-hitter with a quick, quick bat. Like Babe Ruth, he belonged in New York. Like Babe Ruth, money brought him to New York. It was always said in the fifties that Kansas City was the Yankees' major-league farm team. According to Joe McGuff, former sports editor at the *Kansas City Star,* there was, in fact, a sweetheart deal between the Yankees and the Athletics, and it had little to do with baseball. The Yankees and the A's made 16 deals between 1955, when Arnold Johnson bought the A's from the Mack family after Connie's death, and 1960, when Johnson went on to his own reward. That is a very interesting piece of information. Sports news wasn't business news in the late fifties. Baseball was its own country, separate, at least in the public mind, from lawyers, under-the-table deals, and collusion.

Joe McGuff, writing in *Trade Him! 100 Years of Baseball's Greatest Deals,* says Yankee owners Dan Topping and Del Webb set up the deal whereby Arnold Johnson bought the Athletics. Johnson was president of a vending-machine company, Automatic Canteen, and Dan Topping sat on the board of directors. All this might be casual enough, especially for the fifties, when the business of America was only business—and even conceding the fact that Johnson said he knew little about baseball and cared less—but Johnson and Topping's dealings extended beyond Automatic Canteen. Johnson bought Yankee Stadium and Blues Stadium (in Kansas City) from Webb and Topping. Johnson then sold the land under Yankee Stadium to the Knights of Columbus and leased the ground and the stadium to the Yankees so that they wouldn't have to pay real-estate taxes. Now, of course, all that George Steinbrenner needs to do to avoid his rent is threaten to move to New Jersey. In the fifties the game was different. No one pretended owners didn't make money.

So the 16 deals, all in New York's favor, were conducted by an owner making money with and for the Yankee owners. A major-league farm was a useful commodity in the fifties, when the bonus rule prohibited a player who received more than $4,000 from playing in the minor leagues for two years. Bonus boys sat on major-league benches for two years, unless a team had a major-league farm. Both Ralph Terry and Clete Boyer were seasoned in Kansas City and then sent to the big club.

Even though Maris's arrival in New York was a matter of those "interlocking directorates" we used to hear about in the 1960s, he came to New York to rendezvous with the center of Saturday night in 1961, and no man since 1938 has been so close to the eyeball of fate. It took everyone by surprise. Roger Maris had never hit 40 home runs or higher than .283. I have an old baseball magazine that has a picture of Rocky Colavito on the cover and a feature titled "Can Colavito Clout 60 in '60?" The question, of course, was rhetorical. The answer was, "Of course not." No one expected Colavito or anyone but Mantle or Mays to come near 60 in 1960. Mays, in fact, had his chance in '58 and '59 when

48

the Giants played in Seals Stadium, a minor-league park, and *Sport* magazine editorialized that any record set there ought not to count because of the easy home-run dimensions; but Mays hit only 29 and 34 homers in those two seasons. Nobody expected Roger Maris to clout 61 in '61. But back to the asterisk:

What did Roger Maris do in game 154?

He hit number 59 in the third inning, off Milt Pappas. No man other than Babe Ruth had hit more home runs in a season. Jimmy Foxx hit 58 in 1932, and so did Greenberg in 1938. Hank had six games left when he hit number 58, but later said the pressure got to him, and all he could muster was a long foul ball. Maris had come to Baltimore, birthplace of Ruth, and outdone every man but the native son.

"What happened in game 154?" is a good question because it focuses on the most dramatic single-season record chase of all time.

It's a good question because it can't be looked up in the *Encyclopedia;* and it isn't a sucker question, a who-cares piece of one-upmanship, like who holds the International League record for doubles, or who was the starting pitcher for the 1911 St. Louis Browns in their home opener? This is a research question. Unless you were there, you have to go to a library and read old newspapers. I like a question that requires a trip to the microfilm room, to one of those gray tepees where the past appears like a mirage on a gritty metal wall. A walk through the past is good for the soul.

The front page of *The New York Times* for Thursday, September 21, 1961, had a story—not a headline story, but a solid two-column piece at the bottom of page one—announcing that Maris hadn't hit 60 but had hit number 59 in 154 games, so the citizens of Gotham could rest easy that the past had escaped the present.

The sports section was a wealth of information. Only 21,032 attended the game. It was a midweek day game, and it had rained the night before. Perhaps the overnight rain kept the crowd down, but considering what was at stake that Wednesday afternoon at Memorial Stadium, the turnout seems modest. Mickey Mantle didn't play because he had a cold—he hadn't played the night before, but Mantle had only 52 homers and was out of the hunt. His season-long presence was crucial for Maris, and undoubtably kept Roger from being walked out of the the record (Maris received no intentional walks in 1961), but when Maris faced destiny in game 154, he had Yogi Berra batting behind him. The game had no bearing on the pennant race. The Tigers challenged until a Labor Day series in New York when they were hammered out of the race; so the late-September home-run feats of Mantle and Maris were done without the pressure or inspiration of a pennant race.

Maris faced Milt Pappas in the first inning and hit a soft fly to rookie Earl Robinson in right. It's appropriate that Maris faced Pappas. Both men became outcasts. Maris received a flourish of publicity in 1985 because he was dying of cancer. The Yankees had him throw out the first ball on opening day, and Roger was finally cheered. Milt Pappas has heard only silence. He's remembered simply as the bait the Orioles used to get Frank Robinson, even though he had a better career record than Don Drysdale. No one would ever have known this except Pappas brought it to light the year Drysdale was elected to the Hall of Fame, and he wasn't even on the ballot. Pappas's lifetime record was 209–164, Drysdale's 209–166. When I read this in *Baseball Digest,* I didn't believe it, so I went to the *Encyclopedia* and there it was in black and white.

Numbers don't lie, but they can be sadly irrelevant. There's the matter of quality of wins. Most of Drysdale's were in the heat of pennant races. Pappas was in only one race—the Baby Bird run at the Yanks in '60. He was 10–8 for the division-winning Braves in '69, but this only reinforces his invisibility. That was the Met year, and most people have to stop to remember who they played in the playoffs. Milt is remembered only in Trivia: for winning 200 games while never winning 20 (Jerry Reuss accomplished this in 1988), for coming within one strike of a perfect game against the Padres in 1972, and for surrendering Roger Maris's 59th home run.

So Maris, who had his troubles with baseball present,* squared off against Milt Pappas, who would have his troubles with baseball's memory, in front of 21,000 intrepid Baltimore fans. The second time up, Maris homered over the 380-foot sign in right on a 2–1 pitch. The *Times* called it a "beautifully arched shot." Maybe it was. I remember Maris's homers as intermediate-range line drives that got out quickly. Mantle hit cathedral shots. ("Uh-

51

oh, an upper-deck job for Mantle," Phil Rizzuto used to say in that wonderful New York City summertime voice.)

Can you imagine being there and knowing that Roger Maris had three more at-bats and was only one swing behind Babe Ruth? I didn't think Maris could break the record in 154 games. I thought God would protect Babe Ruth, and I was a confirmed fourteen-year-old atheist. Even a Yankee-hater couldn't hate the Yankees of Ruth and Gehrig. Those Yankees were giants from an age of heroes that predated the corporate monotony of Casey Stengel's perennial winners, just as now the 1950s Yankees dwarf the egocentric free-agent crew of the 1970s and their plastic Stadium. Mickey Mantle wasn't Joe DiMaggio, Joe DiMaggio wasn't Lou Gehrig, and Lou Gehrig wasn't Babe Ruth. I sure as hell didn't want Roger Maris trespassing on any of them.

Maris hit number 59 in the third inning. With six innings to go, the son of a bitch was eyeball-to-eyeball with God.

Imagine being there. Even if you were rooting for Ruth and hated Maris, you had to admire the guts of this poor bastard who was chasing the most sacred record in American sports, in the least sacred of American cities, under the most intense media scrutiny, who had come to Ruth's hometown and hit a home run in the third inning! Maris faced Pappas with the presence of Babe Ruth hanging almost palpably in the Baltimore air, and by God, the second time up, the son of a bitch hit one.

If you were squirming in a bleacher seat, would you have switched horses and started rooting for

Maris? He got three more at-bats. Three. The magical baseball number. Three. The fateful number of strikes and outs. Three. Babe Ruth's number. Three. The basic numerical unit of the game itself. Three. The number of God's Person. Three at-bats in Baltimore for unrivaled, unqualified, un-asterisked immortality. And Maris had already hit one, so he wasn't paralyzed like Greenberg. Maris was oiled and ready.

In the fourth inning he faced Dick Hall, the six-foot-six Swarthmore graduate, a man who liked to refer to himself as "baseball's resident intellectual." Hall faced Maris twice that afternoon. It's ironic that a "resident intellectual" from a pansy college should be called on to protect the most sacred record in American sports, but baseball is stranger than fiction. I met Dick Hall at a SABR convention in Baltimore, and all he talked about was eating bugs in the bullpen and playing practical jokes on Moe Drabowsky. Whether his edge came from bugs or books, Hall struck out Maris in the fourth.

In the seventh, Roger's penultimate chance at un-asterisked greatness and equality with the palpable presence in the Baltimore skies, fate tantalized Roger Maris in a way no other slugger has ever been tantalized. Batting in game 154, with 59 homers, Maris hit one into the right-field bleachers ten feet foul. What an unbearable irony and trick of destiny: to come so close and go foul. Who doesn't identify with that?

The at-bat wasn't over. Hall could have walked him and gotten off the hook Tracy Stallard is forever hung from. It's an interesting question whether it's better to be remembered for giving up a homer or forgotten for not giving it up. Is it better to be Ralph Branca or Dick Hall? Better a bum or forgotten? Infamy or oblivion? It was Hall's best against Maris's best and the ball went foul. Hall still could have walked him but didn't. Maris hit another long fly that got held up in the wind and caught by Earl Robinson in front of the railing in right center field. Years later, Roger told Tony Kubek, "The damn ball just died."

Maris got one more chance. We all like to think we get one more chance, and Roger got his. Hoyt Wilhelm was on the mound—Hoyt Wilhelm, recent Cooperstown inductee, top relief pitcher in the American League, and owner of perhaps the most devilishly unpredictable knuckleball of all time. Is there a better emblem for the tricks of fate than the uncertain fancies of the knuckleball? Maris got his last chance in the ninth. There were two out and nobody on base—it was just Maris, myth, and the knuckler: Maris, Ruth, and that tantalizing, flickering, 70-mile-an-hour pitch. I suspect that if any of us ever gets a chance to swing for the world, fame, and paradise, like Maris in game 154, we will get a devious, freakish, unpredictable pitch. Maris was fooled, "badly fooled" the *Times* said, and hit a check-swing roller. Wilhelm fielded it and Maris was out. Roger went on to tie and break Ruth's record, but September 20, game 154, Milt Pappas, Dick Hall, and the knuckleball, are the real story for me.

Never let it be said that Americans don't revere the past. Never let it be said we worship only the most obvious forms of success. No less an observer than Arthur Daley wrote in the *Times,* "The homeric feats this season of Maris and Mickey Mantle . . . have shown that the Babe's 60 is within range of mere mortals." The eminent Mr. Daley missed his point. No one in baseball—the public, me, or, I suspect, even Mr. Daley—wanted the Babe's record broken, especially by a "mere mortal." Even in a country where the biggest lover, the biggest drunk, and the biggest fighter can't find the center of Saturday night, certain things are sacred.

Rookie Questions

THERE is no major record held by a rookie. It's revealing to see just how far the rookie marks are below the single-season marks. This is a testament to how difficult the game is to learn and play. Gale Sayers scored 22 touchdowns for the Bears in his rookie year. That is a remarkable record, accomplished in 14 games, not 16, and the NFL wasn't a shoestring, leather-helmeted sideshow in 1965. It did have direct competition from the AFL, but pro football, and the Green Bay Packers, were beginning to move squarely into the national psyche, and a rookie from Kansas, who wasn't even the Bears' first draft pick, broke Lenny Moore's record of 19. This also happened in the NBA. Another Jayhawk, Wilt Chamberlain, after a stint with the Harlem Globe-Trotters, annihilated the scoring record by averaging 37.6, when no one else had averaged 30. These are significant records. They tell us something about the relative difficulty of perfection in these games. There seems to be something essentially physical about football and basketball. Finesse, skill, training, and savvy don't count as much as a phenomenal body, or extraordinary ability.

Until 1987 no rookie had ever hit 40 home runs, let alone 60, and home runs are certainly the baseball equivalent of points scored and touchdowns. No baseball rookie had ever done anything approaching what Sayers and Chamberlain did in their sports.

Mark McGwire's 49 rookie home runs are truly remarkable. Men are getting stronger as weight training is perfected, but to break the old record by 11? That's 30 percent more, which is an amazing differential to break a record by. Can you imagine Maris's record being broken by 11? That would require hitting 72 home runs! Forty-nine rookie home runs may not be bettered in our lifetimes.

Who holds the National League rookie home-run record?

This question puts in perspective how difficult McGwire's feat was. McGwire had 33 at the All-Star break—it's hard to imagine a rookie ever doing that again. The media, as they always do, started ballyhooing a run at 61. This was foolish, as anyone familiar with rookie homer totals knows. No rookie had ever hit more than 38, so it wasn't realistic to expect one to hit 50, let alone 61. Much more should have been made of McGwire's beating the rookie mark and less in comparing him to Roger Maris.

The National League record is shared by two men: one a superstar and the other a good player. It's interesting to speculate which type McGwire will be. I suspect the former. One of the co-recordholders is easy. Frank Robinson belted 38 homers as a skinny twenty-year-old on the gangbusting '56 Redlegs. Here's a piece of trivia that reveals something about the times. What club changed its nickname for political reasons? Even though the Cincinnati Reds were sixty years older than the Soviet Union, the team felt obligated to change its name during the McCarthy era. That Cincinnati team had an appropriately John Foster Dulles offense. It was the Bomb and the threat of the Bomb. Frank Robinson and a collection of white sluggers —the mighty Klu, Wally Post, Gus Bell, Ed Bailey, et al.—hit 221 homers, which is the NL team record. The '47 Giants also hit 221 in the pull-it-it's-out Polo Grounds. Here's an interesting question: How many of those forgotten Giant sluggers can you name? Johnny Mize hit 51 and has gone on to Cooperstown, but who else helped put that astounding total together? (A clue—one of them was Jewish.) This question admirably demonstrates that if a team doesn't win the pennant, or dramatically lose it, neither numbers nor playing in New York can save it from oblivion. (The Giant sluggers who contributed to the team's 221 homers by hitting more than 13 homers each were Sid Gordon, Willard Marshall, Bobby Thompson, and Walker Cooper. Gordon was Jewish.)

The other rookie home-run hitter is Wally Berger, who hit 38 in 1930, the year Hack Wilson hit 56, and the National League .303. Berger was a right-hand hitter with a pretty swing who played in old Braves Field, where wind, rain, and fog blew off the Charles River over the train tracks and it was hard to hit a home run. Berger never hit more than 34 after 1930, but that swing and spacious Braves Field are remembered a little longer because of the rookie record.

What is the highest rookie batting average?

This is a look-it-up, but the question shows the difficulty of being a big-league rookie. There is some subtlety here. What is a rookie? Joe Reichler's *Great All-Time Baseball Record Book* (with a title like that and the new Yankee Stadium on the cover, one is ashamed to be seen with the thing, but it's an excellent book) lists the highest NL rookie average as George Watkins of the Cardinals in the Year of the Deluge, 1930, at .373. By the way, if the fact the league hit .303 doesn't convince you that statistics from 1930 should be taken with a grain of hindsight, bear in mind that the National League season record for home runs and RBIs (Hack Wilson: 56 and 190), rookie home runs and RBIs (Berger: 38 and 119), rookie slugging (Watkins .621), and rookie batting average were all set in 1930.

Dwight Gooden set the National League rookie record for strikeouts in 1984 by fanning 276 at age 19. Who set the AL rookie mark and with how many? (Answers to this and subsequent questions in this chapter are to be found at the end of the chapter, on page 78.)

Watkins batted 391 times and walked 24 times, which wouldn't qualify him for the batting title now, but in 1930 the requirements were looser. In 1926, Bubbles Hargrave won the title (one of only two catchers to do so—the other was Ernie Lombardi) with a mere 326 at-bats, and Debs Garms, of the Pirates, won the batting championship in 1940 at .355, with 358 at-bats. Joe Jackson batted 571 times in his first full season, 1911, and batted .408, but Joe had played in 30 games prior to that year, and even though those 30 games were spread out over three seasons, he was not considered a rookie. Jackson's .408 is the most impressive batting feat by a first-year player. He never hit .400 again.

One of the rarest occurrences is a pure rookie shortstop on a pennant winner. Name a shortstop who had never appeared in a major-league game before leading a team to the pennant. It happened in the 1930s.

What rookie had the most RBIs? This question demonstrates how answers make questions more interesting. Look-up questions are, at best, moderately interesting. It's worth knowing what rookie had the highest average, if only to know what that average is. The name George Watkins doesn't summon up memories for me, though had I been alive, or young, or very happy when the twenty-eight-year-old strode on the scene, I might feel differently. The RBI question is better. The answer is Ted Williams, who knocked in 145 runs in 1939 as a twenty-year-old rookie. That figure, too, is a long way from the single-season record, but no rookie has done better. It adds to Williams's legend to know that he holds that record. Williams holds two other rookie records that aren't so well known. He walked 107 times, which is the major-league rookie record, and slugged .609, which was the AL record until Mark McGwire slugged .618 in '87. Walt Dropo, the lumbering six-foot-five first baseman of the 1950 Red Sox (last team to hit .300), had the second-best rookie RBI total with 144, and I'm glad that Moose or Snowshoes, as he was aptly called, didn't break Ted's record, though there is something satisfying about a rookie record held by someone who never did anything else.

Rookies are the lifeblood of the game. What's more exciting than a good young player? A promising rookie has a touch of the great and a whisper of immortality until curve balls and a second trip around the league demonstrate how rare a good one really is. Seeing the locals come up with a young player is enough to restore my faith in everything from New England weather to capitalism. It's as close to getting something for nothing as those of us who don't work for the federal government are likely to see. Good prospects make one forget bad trades (Danny Cater for Sparky Lyle—Mother of God!) and blown leads, and make a new season really new.

The best decade for rookies has to be the 1950s. Almost every year of that flush decade saw the arrival not only of a Hall of Famer, but of someone to compare to the all-time greats. Willie Mays and Mickey Mantle came up in 1951, which was a pretty good year for center fielders. Both played for pennant winners in the media capital, but only

Mays was Rookie of the Year. Who was the American League Rookie of the Year in 1951?

The answer is Gil McDougald, the nice guy, all-purpose Yankee spare part, and despoiler of Herb Score. What could be more appropriate for that repressed, buttoned-down decade than to pick the quiet nice guy and miss the genius?

Talk of rookies leads to Rookies of the Year. Fans have a weakness for awards as well as statistics. Both aid memory and fuel arguments. The Rookie of the Year Award started in 1947 as a way, I suspect, of honoring Jackie Robinson, who as the Rookie of His Race was made to feel like an outsider in all the overt and insidious ways America had been devising for three hundred years. No rookie ever deserved the award more. No rookie ever had the off-the-field impact of Robinson, and few have equaled his on-field accomplishments. Jackie Robinson had speed and power and ran the bases with head-down, spikes-up, full-contact abandon. Jackie was twenty-eight, a college man, World War II vet, and former professional football player. His knees were banged up, and he literally carried the hopes of a whole race on his back. It could not have been an easy year. What position did Jackie Robinson play his rookie year? He played first base, moving to second with the arrival of Gil Hodges a year later.

There was only one award for both leagues the first two years. Al Dark won it over Larry Doby the second year, which is like having an award that Martin Luther King, Jr., could win one year and George Wallace the next. Dark is *not* the answer to a famous answerless trivia question: Who caught a touchdown pass from Y. A. Tittle and hit a home run off Sandy Koufax? No one accomplished those feats (Dark and Tittle both attended LSU but not at the same time), but like the belief that George Halas preceded Babe Ruth in right field for the Yankees (he didn't, Sammy Vick did), or that Honus Wagner knocked Ty Cobb unconscious in a play at second in the 1909 World Series (he didn't, but the collective sense of retribution wouldn't let the story die), the notion has passed into lore. Perhaps there's a need that underlies Trivia for information to be related. Perhaps we are all looking for a unified field theory of information, and our deepest need is for everything to make sense. Under the madness of Trivia may be the sane and hopeful desire to believe that information and life itself make sense, or could make sense, if we knew enough, or could find the pattern.

In 1949 the rookie award was given in both leagues. Who were the first simultaneous winners? This is a look-it-up, but a significant one. The winners were Roy Sievers, a slugger in the grand old slew-footed white 1950s power mold, and Don Newcombe, the first of only four black pitchers to be Rookie of the Year.

It's easy to make fun of awards, but Rookies of the Year are a source of practically endless delight. We, of course, have hindsight to highlight the more dubious choices, but the Rookie of the Year Awards have been as foolish as the Nobel Prize for Literature. Gil McDougald won over Mickey Mantle; Sinclair Lewis beat James Joyce. Don Schwall was picked over Carl Yastrzemski; Pearl Buck got the award and F. Scott Fitzgerald didn't. Curt Blefary beat Paul Blair; John Steinbeck won, Vladimir Nabokov did not.

It's easy to make jokes about Rookies of the Year and great players who started in the same season, but who knows? Maybe Wally Moon looked like a better hitter to your average card-carrying member of the BBWAA than the young Henry Aaron. Aaron hit .280 with 13 homers in '54, and unless you noticed his wrists and bat speed (only the most important items in judging a young hitter), maybe Wally Moon's .304 and 12 homers looked like a better bet. I think it's safe to say that the writers a year later who picked Bill Virdon over a twenty-one-year-old Roberto Clemente (who hit .255 with five homers in 124 games) weren't necessarily a "lot of prejudiced chuckleheads" as Huck Finn says, because Virdon hit .281 with 17 home runs, and was also an excellent outfielder. That Virdon finished his solid career with a lifetime BA of .267, and Clemente finished his great one at .317, was not something a writer could figure out any more than he could have known all hell would break loose when a truckdriver from Memphis appeared on "The Ed Sullivan Show."

The great ones are not always passed over. Mays got the award, and so did Frank Robinson (he did tie the rookie home-run mark; like McGwire, he was hard to overlook), Luis Aparicio (also in '56, making it a year like '67; both Rookies of the Year are or will be in the Hall of Fame), and Willie McCovey won in '59, even though he appeared in only 52 games. McCovey hit .354 with 13 homers and 38

RBIs in his brief rookie campaign, and the Giants had done it again. They seemed to have an endless supply of great black and Latin players: Mays in '51, Cepeda in '58, McCovey in '59, Marichal in '60. They also brought up Felipe Alou, Willie Kirkland, and Leon Wagner. The Giants brought up more good black players during that period than the entire American League. They outfiftied the fifties with that parade of sluggers, but there was a more important rookie than Willie McCovey in 1959.

He didn't win the award, and his stats don't compare to McCovey's. There's little chance this gentleman will make the Hall of Fame, and he's already washed out as a manager and broadcaster, but he was ahead of his time. Maury Wills played the AstroTurf game before AstroTurf.

The 1962 season saw a record broken that had seemed as secure as Ruth's 60 home runs. Ty Cobb's 96 stolen bases was a mark from a distant past when men wore pancake gloves, the World Series was fixed, and fans came to the ballpark by horse. Maury Wills terrorized the National League with a weapon from the dead-ball era. His base-stealing numbers hadn't been seen since Germany had a Kaiser and Russia a Czar, but sometimes the future comes disguised as the past. There were inklings of what was to come in '59, when Wills stole seven bases in 83 games, but in '62 Wills exploded.

A man who never hit more than six home runs in a season was suddenly as important as Willie Mays. This is as amazing as Roger Maris challenging Babe Ruth. Wills simply ran all over the fifties' stereotypical, lumbering, home-run-hitting catchers.

(Remember Smoky Burgess, Ed Bailey, Gene Oliver, and Del Crandall? They might as well have been trying to throw out something from outer space.) The Dodgers reinvented the art of manufacturing runs when you can't hit. Wills shook up catchers, infielders, and pitchers. He forced catchers to be able to field again. No longer could a club use an over-the-hill white slugger as catcher. The game, in the National League, was no longer so simple.

I know its statistically chic to deny the value of the stolen base. At the Society for American Baseball Research national convention, when the best, brightest, and craziest baseball fans in America get together for three days of unmitigated mathematical one-upmanship, arguments about the value of the stolen base (either instigated by or aimed at Bill James) raise more hackles than any other subject except possibly range factor (a Jamesian attempt to create a meaningful defensive statistic).

Maybe it is possible to prove statistically that a stolen base is worth .2 percent of a run, and calculate how many times a team must steal successfully to warrant even attempting the tactic, but that doesn't account for the shock of Maury Wills in 1962, when fans and players alike were still lumbering in the spiritual 1950s, and Wills simply tore defenses apart.

Before Maury Wills stole 50 bases in 1960, who was the last National Leaguer to steal 50?

In the *1986 Baseball Abstract* Bill James does an excellent job of demonstrating the drawbacks of stealing bases. He reports that a National League umpire said, "Wills had cost the Dodgers the pennant with his running. . . . He had seen Junior Gilliam take too many pitches . . . just to allow Wills to steal." Bill James is, in my opinion, the most interesting baseball mind in the country, and his critique of base-stealing may be right if one looks at the long history of the stolen base, but it's not right about Maury Wills in 1962. Numbers are wonderful, but they aren't reality. They are symbols—marvelous symbols—but they are not the mind of God. James has revolutionized the way fans look at statistics, reputations, and in the superb *Historical Baseball Abstract* even the past itself, but sometimes the schemes of genius fail to snare reality. In 1962, Wills was a visitor from the future. He was playing the game the way it would be played twenty years later, and he was devastating. His impact was much greater than that of his fellow rookie Willie McCovey.

Babe Ruth started the power revolution, but Maury Wills, who didn't win Rookie of the Year, popularized speed, and speed meant defense and athletic ability. Sixties baseball was faster and blacker, and pitching dominated. What two men, who were 8–6 and 3–5 in '59, were the most dominating players of the next decade? One was a rookie, the other was wild. Sandy Koufax and Bob

Gibson could have gone the way of Karl Spooner and Ryne Duren, but they found control, and ballparks changed with the building of Chavez Ravine. The most important rookie of 1962 was neither Ken Hubbs (first Mormon to be Rookie of the Year) nor the infinitely more talented Lou Brock, but Chavez Ravine itself. The game on the field is defined by the shape of the field, and home runs were not hit in Dodger Stadium in appreciable numbers until the plate was moved closer to the fences in the late seventies.

Koufax started pitching in a new ballpark in '62, Gibson in '66, and both of them thrived in places where it was hard to hit a home run. It was hard to hit anywhere they pitched, but the trend toward pitching, speed, and defense started in 1959, when Koufax and Wills's team won the World Series (the first team of the decade to win without a super-slugger—either a slugger emeritus like DiMaggio in 1950, an apprentice immortal like Mantle in '51, '52, and '53, a bona fide genius like Mays or the young Henry Aaron, or a hard-hitting lineup such as the Dodgers had until they broke Brooklyn's heart—and choose the future's base paths over the musclebound past).

The rookie doubles record is 52 by Dodger Johnny Frederick in 1929. The AL mark, however, was set by a player who is still active. He looked like a Hall of Famer for a few years, but has settled into being just "good." Name him.

What could be more emblematic of the change from fifties to sixties baseball than the fate of 1960's NL Rookie of the Year? Poor Frank Howard. He had been brought up in the era of slugging, and had all the slugger's tools. Was anyone ever so well prepared for one decade and then cast into another? Think of Frank Howard in Ebbets Field. He would have been another Ralph Kiner. The Dodgers traded Howard and others to the Senators for Claude Osteen—exchanging bulk for pitching, the fifties for the sixties—and won two pennants. Howard was a fine hitter for Washington, but, stuck on that team, he might as well have been the next Steve Bilko. Howard is the answer to a question that time has eroded: Who was the only man in either league to hit 40 homers in 1968, the year when no one in the slugger-rich NL hit more than 36, and the AL batting champ had the most humble average since organized baseball began, that summer when Custer lost his scalp? Frank Howard hit 44 home runs the year nobody hit anything. Had the Dodgers stayed in Brooklyn, Frank Howard would be in the Hall of Fame.

A good rookie question is a question that leads to a man who changed, or who epitomized a change in the way the game was played. Any question that

leads to a career that saw an unbreakable record
challenged or broken is also a good question. Unbreakable records are essential to our conception of
ourselves as fans. We need standards, and beyond
the standards, we need boundaries. Sixty home
runs is the boundary of magic. Thirty wins is magical (even if Denny McLain did it). A lifetime BA over
.330 is magical. A baseball fan, unlike the practi-
tioners of other religions, immediately knows the
miraculous when he sees it. Roger Clemens struck
out 20 men in a nine-inning game in 1986, and the
Boston Globe informed the sporting public that this
hadn't been done in the previous 150,000 major-
league baseball games. Let each fan conjure with
that figure. Feats that may never occur again are
essential to fans. We like to think we've seen things
that won't happen again. We need the great. It legit-
imizes us. It lets us think we haven't wasted the
colossal amount of time and imagination we've
spent on baseball. The extraordinary redeems the
mundane, just as humor can, and we adore the idea
that we've seen the best. To have seen Babe Ruth or
Ted Williams is better than having heard the chimes
at midnight.

Maury Wills is the transitional figure between
the supermen of the fifties, the running sluggers—
Aaron, Mays, Mantle, and Frank Robinson—and the
line-drive, stolen-base, AstroTurf game of the
1980s. Wills broke an unbreakable record. He stole
98 bases in 154 games—Cobb's record was 96, so
baseball didn't have to do a dance of cognitive dissonance and behave as though Cobb's record were

still the record. Stealing a hundred broke a conceptual barrier. I've always thought that a hundred stolen bases, along with John Kennedy's assassination, signaled the breakup of the fifties' world of sluggers, big cars, falsies, and switchblades, as the game of white slew-feet and a handful of black supermen became Pete Rose, relief pitching, and phony turf.

Wills's significance has been dimmed by his personality, both as a manager and broadcaster. He doesn't seem able to get along with anybody, and was notably ungracious when thirty-four-year-old Lou Brock broke his stolen-base record in 1974. Maybe all men hate to see their records broken; few, however, carp in public. Only Ted Williams seems above it all. I believe Ted when he says he wishes "some son of a bitch" would hit .400 so reporters won't ask his opinion when somebody gets close. I know I hope no one hits .400, because I want to think I've seen the best and chronicled my wasted time with a glimpse of perfection. Maury Wills isn't Ted Williams, and the stolen-base record was his sole truck with immortality. It's easy to lose sympathy for a man whose vanity may resemble our own.

Who was AL Rookie of the Year in Don Mattingly's rookie season? This may be the award question of the nineties. I think your gut tells you who the best player in baseball is. He's the man you're most afraid of when the game is on the line. Mattingly is that man for me. His lifetime BA is .327 and he hits home runs and doubles, and set the

Yankee season-hit mark with 238 in '86. Mattingly's stats and even his way of standing at the plate are strikingly reminiscent of Stan Musial. Ron Kittle was AL Rookie of the Year in 1983. Kittle hit 35 home runs and had 100 RBIs while Mattingly, who played in 91 games, had four homers and 32 RBIs. Kittle deserved the award, but that selection will look more like Wally Moon as the years go by.

We know about DiMaggio, Rose, and Keeler. Jimmy Williams of the Pirates hit in 29 straight games in 1899. This mark stood until Benito Santiago hit in 34 games in '87. This, like McGwire's homer mark, may last the rest of our lives. Santiago's 34 also set another record. What was it?

Rookie questions should parallel trends in the game, and one of the most significant recent changes has been the dominance of relief pitchers. Who was the first relief pitcher to be Rookie of the Year? The year was 1952 and the man was 15–4 with 15 saves for a pennant-winning team. Another relief pitcher wouldn't be selected for 34 years. The first was Joe Black, one of 11 Dodgers who have been Rookie of the Year, but the only reliever until Todd Worrell. Nineteen eighty-six was a good year for rookie relievers. The record for appearances was set by hard-throwing Texas reliever Mitch Williams, who is the only pitcher I've seen throw three fastballs by Wade Boggs. Ranger Dale Mohorcic tied a major-league record and set a rookie mark by appearing in 13 consecutive games. Todd Worrell set a rookie record with 36 saves, and certainly deserved the award. This record, however, is in jeopardy, as relief specialists now come straight from the minors and are in great demand.

Rookies are notoriously hard to judge. What 1982 rookie hit .349 in part of a season (338 at-bats), and wasn't even considered for the award because he didn't hit home runs, ran the bases poorly (still does), and didn't field his position well? That fine BA looked like a fluke. Rookie averages, especially in partial seasons, can be deceiving. Dave Stapleton, the only man to lower his average for seven consecutive years, hit .321 his first year, so Wade Boggs's .349 was greeted with skepticism. The next year Boggs hit .361 but still wasn't selected to the All-Star team. It took him four years to be an All-Star. Now Pete Rose says Boggs may be the only hitter in either league who won't go into a prolonged slump. Boggs isn't the first Red Sox star overlooked for Rookie of the Year. Yaz didn't win either.

The American League had two Rookies of the Year in Rickey Henderson's first year, 1979: Alfredo Griffin and John Castino. They hit .287 and .285 respectively, which, regardless of runs and RBIs, let alone Secondary Average, Total Average, Overall Winning Average, or any of the new statistics let out of Bill James's box, is usually enough to win the award. Henderson hit .274 and stole 33 bases in 83 games. Griffin and Castino played more important positions, but those selections are destined to join Gil McDougald and Kittle.

Tim Raines and Vince Coleman didn't have

Henderson and Boggs's problem. They each broke the rookie theft record and won the award. This is appropriate because we live in an age of base sprinters. Raines broke the rookie mark in the strike season of '81 by stealing 71 bases in 88 games. Given a full season, he might have challenged Henderson's 130. Vince Coleman did have a full season and stole 110. The baseball superstar has changed. What do Rickey Henderson, Tim Raines, and Vince Coleman have in common with Willie Mays, Hank Aaron, and Frank Robinson? The answer is nothing. There has been a change. The best black athletes—"best" meaning big as well as superbly coordinated—play killer-in-your-face games. I fear that baseball no longer excites the imagination of the ghetto. Jackie Robinson belongs to the age of Nat "King" Cole and the NAACP. Baseball's stars are middle-class Californians, white college boys, and Latins. There are exceptions like Eric Davis and Dwight Gooden, but there just aren't the number of talented black players that made the last three decades so strong.

Future Rookies of the Year will be lean basesprinters and gym-built musclemen. The season stolen-base record, rookie and major league, will never be unbreakable again. McGwire's home-run record, despite Nautilus machines and free weights, will endure. Home-run records are rarely broken. No rookie before McGwire had hit 40, and only ten men have ever hit 50. It could take another fifty-eight years before McGwire is bettered.

Rookie questions will always be interesting. We all identify with early promise. Who doesn't remember the feeling the world is all before him?

Answers to questions in the preceding chapter:

- The AL rookie strikeout record is held by the ill-fated Herb Score, who had 245 in 1955.

- Frank Crosetti of the 1932 Yankees had not played a game in the major leagues prior to that season.

- The last NL player to steal 50 bases before Maury Wills was Max Carey, who stole 51 in 1923.

- The AL rookie doubles record is 47 by Fred Lynn in his remarkable rookie year, 1975.

- Benito Santiago's 34-game hitting streak is the longest by a catcher.

Worsts and Forgotten Selves

FREUD and my high school Latin teacher liked to say that memory is selective, but why do we take such delight in the ridiculous? Why do blunders, disasters, "worsts," and the egregiously awful make their way into lore along with epic moments? Part of the pleasure, I think, is a natural enjoyment of the worst, which counterbalances praise of the best; and some of us, I fear, have a streak of anarchy and thumb our noses at all sorts of authority, even the authority of excellence. There is, after all, a certain pleasure to be had in seeing a comic pratfall in one act of a tragedy, and a great soliloquy in the next. The awful also helps put the excellent in perspective. In catechism, unlike history, the first never loses sight of the last. "Worsts," as well as "bests," reveal the difficulty of the game.

What is the lowest number of RBIs a man batting over 500 times has had in a season?

This is another way of saying, "How ineffectual can a player be?" The answer is 12 by Enzo Hernandez, a light-hitting shortstop for the San Diego Padres who went to bat 549 times in 1971. Ray Oyler, one of the weakest-hitting shortstops of all time (.175 lifetime BA in 596 games), drove in 12 runs for the Tigers in '68, but Oyler batted only 215 times.

What's the highest ERA for a twentieth-century pitcher who worked over 150 innings in a season?

If you guess it happened in 1930, the year the National League BA was .303 and the New York Giants hit .319, you would be correct. A good bet for a worst is always Philadelphia, and the Phillies were the worst team in the league in the year of the jackrabbit ball. The Lords of baseball jazzed up the ball in 1930 (it had also been done in 1920) in the hope that slugging would attract lean Depression fans the way Babe Ruth and high averages had delivered their fuller selves the previous decade, and the Phillies lost 102 games while the staff had an ERA of 6.71. This amazingly bad team not only had the pitcher with the worst ERA in the twentieth century who worked over 150 innings, but the worst two! Les Sweetland had a 7.71 ERA, which is the worst, and Claude Willoughby had a 7.59 ERA. These infamous marks may never be topped.

The '30 Phillies hit .315, second highest in baseball history. They weren't dull, just terrible. Steve Blass, the pitcher who fell from grace with the plate, went, without injury, from a 19–8 with a 2.49 ERA in '72 to 3–9 in '73 with an 9.85 ERA, but pitched only 88 innings. Blass simply lost the ability to pitch. His career ended so quickly it was hard not to feel he had secretly been one of us who got found out.

What twentieth-century pitcher lost the most games in a season?

This question isn't as much of a hoot as Sweetland's and Willoughby's ERAs. It's difficult to lose games in large numbers and stay in the big leagues, let alone stay in a starting rotation. Many more pitchers have won 20 than lost 20 and no one has lost 30 in this century. Vic Willis of the woeful '05 Boston Braves lost 29, and it took a pitcher as good as Willis to lose that many. Willis, who had an excellent curveball, lost 20 twice, but won 20 eight times, including four years in a row for the Pirates.

The ignominious is also a clue to the way the game is played. Who struck out the most times in a season?

Bobby Bonds fanned an incredible 189 times in 1970, and he was a lead-off hitter. This record, like the stolen-base record, is in danger of being broken every year. Pete Incaviglia struck out 185 times his rookie season. Jose Canseco fanned 175 times. Bo Jackson was headed for 200 his first season, but played less as the year ended. The career strikeout kings are almost all post-1945. We live in an era of the Big Bang and the Big Whiff, and this is unfortunate, because nothing slows down a game like a strikeout. Unless a pitcher is a lightning-armed artist like Ryan, Gooden, or Clemens, nothing is as tedious as the intermittent strikeout. When the ball isn't put in play, nothing happens: no fielding, no base-running, not even the possibility of an error. Our grandfathers didn't have the Dave Kingmans and Butch Hobsons to gum up their afternoons.

What is the lowest career batting average?

There's something remarkable about the worst of anything—the homeliest guy, the ugliest woman, the most obnoxious announcer. The lowest career average is more interesting than the lowest season average because any number of men who didn't belong in the big leagues have come close to .000 before sinking back to the minors, but Bill Bergen, a turn-of-the-century catcher, played 11 years, went to bat over 3,000 times, and hit .170. Enzo Hernandez managed a robust-by-comparison .224 career mark. Bergen's .170 is the worst career stat of all time.

There may be more than a rebel's chuckle or a wink at the absurd in our appreciation of the ridiculous. Details, seemingly unrelated and random, can make the past flower. Our memories are a tapestry made of details, fragments, sensations, dreams —everything that we've seen, felt, heard, made up, and remembered—but this tapestry hangs in a dark hall and we never see it all. Catechism, like free association, or dream analysis, momentarily illuminates part of it. When I hear a piece of Trivia, even just a lost and unremembered name from the beginning of my career as a fan, I get a thrill, and the slight but distinct sense of having found another piece of the puzzle.

Who knows what lurks in a name? I once met a man at a party, who, though no longer a fan, had been an American League fanatic between 1948 and 1953. I always talk baseball to strangers because it is a lingua franca, a way to dispense with pretense and redeem ordinary evenings. (One of Trivia's cardinal virtues is that it cuts through bullshit. Ask the next would-be aficionado, or the loudest gent at the bar, to name five men who've won two or more batting titles and have under .300 life averages, and see if that doesn't take his mind off himself for a while. This question is too good to answer immediately. The answer is on page 95.) When the gentleman heard I liked Trivia, he said, "Who played first base for the Yankees in '53 with Joe Collins?" I looked him in the eye and said, "Johnny Mize."

"Don Bollweg," he said, and I was caught between a worldly-wise smile that means "I'll file that away for the next New York-know-it-all," and a wry who-cares shrug. The shrug would have been inappropriate because Bollweg played 43 games at first on a club that won a still-unduplicated five straight World Championships. That five-year reign started with DiMaggio, ended with Mantle, and Casey Stengel platooned and shuffled like a dealer in a high-stakes card game. The one constant, of course, was pitching: Reynolds, Raschi, Lopat, and then a cagy veteran like Sain, a well-traveled vet like Bob Kuzava, an enigma like Tommy Byrne, a rookie master like Whitey Ford, and Yogi Berra to handle them.

So Bollweg didn't play for just anybody. Humble as his contribution may have been, he's more than a name in the Macmillan *Encyclopedia*, like those fellows who played one game in 1887, have only one name, and the sole piece of biographical information is "deceased."

There was something in the way the gentleman said "Don Bollweg" that kept me from filing the name for ammunition. He smiled a half-apologetic but inward smile, and I realized the name meant something he couldn't express any other way. Perhaps at fifteen he had aspired to be Johnny Mize, Casey's "secret weapon," a savvy pro helping a championship team, but knew he was really Don Bollweg, a journeyman footnote to a dynasty, whose name conjures up images of anonymity. I think the question made the guy remember a shade of himself he'd tried to forget, which could be both summoned and hidden by the palimpsest "Bollweg."

I have a question that summons a forgotten self, and it's my favorite question. What teenager hit the most home runs in a season?

For years the teenage homer record was held by Mel Ott, whom John McGraw kept on the Giants for fear a minor-league manager would try to change Ott's unorthodox swing. Mel hit 18 homers at age nineteen. That mark stood until Boston's ill-fated slugger, Tony Conigliaro, hit 24 home runs in 1964, at the age of 19. The next year, Tony became the youngest home-run king when he hit 32 at age twenty. I find the first feat more impressive than the second. Doing anything well, other than the sort of thing memorialized on bathroom walls, at 19, impresses me.

Conigliaro was a hometown boy. He almost signed with the Orioles in '63 but chose the Red Sox because they had been his team. Conigliaro was a local hero, but being a hero in Boston is like being a politician in Boston. Those who attract attention attract controversy. This city likes to create and destroy its heroes, sometimes simultaneously. Ted Williams was detested by a vocal minority until he was old enough to be venerated. Where else could the most charismatic star of his generation come back from a war, hit a home run, and feel obligated to give the French salute to the press box? Where but Boston? Who but Ted Williams?

Tony Conigliaro was the first player of consequence who was about my age. He was only two years older, and when he homered on the first pitch thrown to him at Fenway Park, I had the stunning realization that guys my age were going to be in the big leagues. This is one of those unavoidable rites of passage that put the world in focus. I still think of big-league ballplayers as older than I, when in fact, in a few years, I will be older than all of them. That is another rite.

To my surprise, I discovered that the nineteen-year-old Conigliaro meant as much to me as players had when I was ten. At that age I had attached my ego to a god, Ted Williams, a man with a distinctly scrutable relationship to perfection. Liking Tony C. was different. I was coming out of the doldrums of a nerdy, pimply, cynical, defensive five years, and completely identified with this brash rookie. Nine-teen sixty-four was a great year. The country was rousing itself from some nerdy, pimply years. The Beatles "happened," as they used to say, in January, and never have harbingers of a new world been so quickly recognized. Suddenly there was a new way to look—if you had the nerve—and girls were inter-ested, or not, solely on the basis of the length of your hair.

Like the spirit of that bright year, and that brief, lost mid-sixties time, the rookie crop was in-credibly promising, but their fate, like that of so many of the kids who graduated in '64, lay in disas-ter. Merritt Clifton of the Society for American Baseball Research has pointed out that there may never have been a crop with so much promise and so little fulfillment. I think there were five potential Hall of Famers, and all were hit with severe, and in one case, terrifying injuries. Tony Oliva is the only rookie to win a batting title. Even Cobb didn't win until his third year. Oliva won four batting cham-pionships, led in hits five times, and in doubles four times. Bad knees reduced his life average to .304, but that is higher than Willie Mays's or Mickey Man-tle's. Oliva's stats resemble those of my Hall of Fame bête noire, George Kell. Lifetime BA: Oliva, .304; Kell, .306. Hits: Oliva, 1,917; Kell, 2,054. Runs: Oliva, 870; Kell, 881. RBIs: Oliva, 947; Kells, 870. Kell did play third base, an underrepresented posi-tion in the Hall. He is also a broadcaster and in daily contact with many who vote.

Dick Allen was another prodigiously talented '64 rookie. He looked like a successor to Hank

Aaron, a right-hand hitter who just murdered the ball. Allen's problems began with an accident involving the headlight of an antique car he was pushing in the rain. His hand went through the light, and tendons were severed in the left wrist. After that, there were frequent trades, problems with alcohol, the press, and the world in general—all redeemed, briefly but completely, with an MVP in the American League in 1972 under the sympathetic eye of Chuck Tanner.

Rico Carty, second after Felipe Alou in what turned out to be a long line of hard-hitting Dominicans, hit .330 that year, which put him behind only Clemente. Carty was bedeviled by injuries, cultural differences, a year lost to tuberculosis, another to a knee, and even a beating administered by cops in Atlanta. There's nothing like a natural hitter with power, and Allen, Oliva, and Carty all had power. I can't think of a year when three hitters that good came up. Jim Ray Hart also debuted in '64 and might have been a perennial All-Star, but two beanings, one by Bob Gibson, ruined him.

Not every rookie in that star-crossed crop was stopped by injury. Luis Tiant appeared in the middle of the year, pitched a shutout against the Yankees, and went on to win another 228 games. Tiant started as a blazer with a wickedly tailing fastball, but suffered arm problems so severe that the Red Sox got him for nothing in 1971. Few pitchers have come back from injuries as devastating as Tiant's, and even fewer have developed the showman's combination of finesse, guile, and just plain guts that made him a great pitcher in the mid-1970s. Tommy

John was a '64 rookie for Cleveland, went 2–9, and was traded to Chicago. John had the longest career in the class of '64. I never found him likable, but it was nice to know what was state-of-the-art in belt-buckle shenanigans. John, like Tiant, had severe arm problems, and had a tendon from his right forearm transplanted to his left elbow. No doubt, he had to pitch with intelligence and courage, but for me, the Hoosier off-speed slider, farther and farther away from the outside corner, just doesn't compare with Tiant's turn-your-fanny-to-the-hitter, nod-at-the-centerfield-camera, spider-on-the-banana-boat curve that could snap a hitter's jockstrap as it broke over the plate. Tiant ought to be in the Hall of Fame.

None of the rookies in that unlucky crop suffered like Tony C. If our favorite questions are a tapestry we weave to hide and remember, who signifies more than Tony Conigliaro? He was talented. He was brash. He was nineteen. Tony spent his bonus money on a Corvette and cut a rock and roll record. Here's a piece of small-*t* trivia: What was the name of Tony C.'s record? "Playing the Field." John Lennon he was not. The flip side was "Little Red Scooter." If Conigliaro was your first contemporary to bid for stardom, and if you saw his precocious and rash talent as an emblem of your own over-reaching, your own attempts to be brash when you'd been timid, to star where you'd been a spectator, to be sassy and mouthy and full of yourself with an I'll-show-'em exuberance, instead of a sarcastic cynicism, then Tony C. was your man.

He was easy to identify with. This wasn't a young Willie Mays or Frank Robinson. This wasn't a born immortal serving a rookie apprenticeship. Tony wasn't fast. He was a good player who might become a great hitter. He was a good player with a specialty, not a raw genius. He always seemed to be overachieving. He was always pushing and challenging his ability. Tony was a teenager—full of awkward promise, full of himself, full of shit, but young, undeniably, unforgivably, and marvelously young.

Conigliaro was vulnerable—physically vulnerable—and nothing made him so young as this. He had a long, lean, high-school body. He always got hurt. Tony had a young man's desire to impress and irritate. He tried the impossible in a way only an adolescent will. A major-league regular at nineteen? A nonpitching regular? Tony C. was talent stretched to the breaking point. He was a brittle overreacher, and that is almost a definition of adolescence.

Conigliaro's promise was derailed by a Jack Hamilton pitch on a Friday night in August 1967. Toward the end of the Summer of Love, and at the beginning of the home stretch of the wildest pennant race since 1908, with the darkest of dark-horse teams, Conigliaro suffered what would come to be called "a near-fatal beaning." This emblematic adolescent, who had 20 homers and 67 RBIs on August 19, was struck by a pitch below the left eye. Bone fragments went into the eye, almost causing blindness.

The beaning had tragic elements. Conigliaro was a natural fastball hitter—that was his promise of greatness; even when he was nineteen, you couldn't throw one by him—Tony had wrists. He was a natural Fenway hitter. Conigliaro murdered fastballs but had trouble with breaking pitches, especially away, so that's how they pitched him. To compensate, he crowded the plate so that he could reach the outside corner. The answer to this strategy, which must date back to the origin of the game —hell, it dates back to the origin of the species—is to pitch inside. The primordial struggle for home plate, batter standing close, pitcher pushing him back, is as common as dogs snarling over territory. Conigliaro and Hamilton faced off over seventeen inches of rubber, and the former Philly, Tiger, and Met hit him in the face. There's nothing quite like the sound of a man getting beaned. It's a sharp, sickening crack. Conigliaro pulled back and the ball hit flesh and bone.

Nothing is as shocking as blood on a baseball field. Baseball is not a violent game—nicks and scratches, yes, even stitches, but not head wounds. I'll never forget the awful pictures of Herb Score in *Life* magazine after Gil McDougald sent a line drive off Score's face in 1957. *Life*, America's visual bard, had a story with black-and-white photos of Score's stunned face. It was impossible not to ask yourself, Why doesn't this happen all the time? Pitchers stand so close, they throw so hard. Is there a line drive with my name on it?

Baseball isn't bloody. Baseball is green and safe. It has neither the street intimidation of basketball, nor the controlled armageddon of football. Men die playing football—not often, but often enough that no one forgets it. Any player can suffer a career-ending injury on any play, and that shattered leg or torn knee can happen on a legal hit. Baseball is different. Baseball is a green dream that happens on summer nights in safe places in unsafe cities. Home plate is not a killing ground. The game isn't mock warfare or a refereed street fight. What made Tony's beaning tragic was that, like the answer to a good trivia question, it seemed inevitable. He pushed himself. He dared. He stood over the plate.

Conigliaro's career didn't end with the beaning. He may not have been the most likable guy, but he had guts. He tried to come back in '68. I saw him in spring training in '68 at Fort Lauderdale against the Yankees. It was one of the worst days of my life. Conigliaro said his eyes were all right, but you could see they weren't. I forget who pitched for the Yankees. It could have been Stottlemyre, Bahnsen, or Petersen, but it also could have been Joe Verbanic, Dooley Womack, or Thad Tillotson. Whoever he was, Conigliaro missed his practice speed pitches by a foot. I think Tony finally got a hit. If he did, it was luck. Everyone in the springtime stadium, including the Yankees, was pulling for him.

He did come back in '69. Tony hit 20 homers and had 82 RBIs. In '70 he belted 36 homers and had 116 RBIs, second in the league. He later said that despite those impressive figures, his eye wasn't right. The tragedy of his career was that when he had good eyes, he didn't have an adult's strength; and when his six-foot-three frame filled out, he didn't have two eyes. Tony C.'s life has been a fairy tale. There was magic, but there was always a price.

The Red Sox traded him in October 1970. I still find the trade hard to believe. How could a club trade a player who'd been through what Tony had been through? He went to California in exchange for two guys named Tatum, and Doug Griffin, then a minor-leaguer. The Red Sox were trading for pitching and speed, the commodities they couldn't produce, but the deal was a disaster for almost everyone involved. Tony's eyesight deteriorated, and he retired halfway through the '71 season, embittered by the trade. Neither of the Tatums helped the Red Sox, and Doug Griffin did not become a star, though he did have the distinction of once being hit in the head by Nolan Ryan.

In '75, Tony Conigliaro came back again. He was a DH and back in Boston. I saw him on Opening Day. A woman threw roses on the field when Tony came to bat. He singled to right, and George Scott, playing first for the Brewers, shook his hand. That chilly April day saw Boston's two greatest might-have-beens, other than Babe Ruth, as rival DHs. Hank Aaron was back in Milwaukee for the end of his amazing career. Aaron had been in the Boston Braves organization when Lou Perini moved the moribund Braves to Milwaukee in 1953. One Boston team traded Babe Ruth, the other moved out of town before Hank Aaron could register an at-bat. No city has ever been teased like that.

Tony's comeback was brief. He got into 21 games, hit .123 with two home runs, and retired for good. The Sox went on to win the pennant, but not with pitching and speed. They brought up Jim Rice and Fred Lynn, who were the first rookie pair to drive in a hundred runs since Cleveland's Ken Keltner and Jeff Heath in 1938. Conigliaro is the answer to two '75 trivia questions, being one of three men to play on both the '67 and '75 teams, and having been the DH on Opening Day in '75. Otherwise he's as forgotten a part of that club as Tim McCarver, who got into a few early-season games as a reserve catcher.

Tony C.'s dealings with fate weren't over. He became a broadcaster and did TV sports in San Francisco. When the color job on Red Sox telecasts became vacant in 1982, he returned for an audition. Billy Conigliaro, a former Red Sox outfielder, was driving his brother to Logan Airport when Tony suffered a massive heart attack. Billy didn't know that the airport had medical facilities. He drove to Massachusetts General Hospital. The trip, even at the speed Billy must have negotiated it, added four to six oxygenless minutes to Tony's ordeal. He was in a coma for a month and only recently has been able to use a walker and recognize his family. The man who reminds me of a lost adolescent self has had to start again in childhood.

Answer to the question on page 85:

- The five men who won two or more batting titles and have under .300 life averages are Mickey Vernon, Ferris Fain, Pete Runnels, Tommy Davis, and Carl Yastrzemski.

Two-League and Other-League Questions

THE most striking feature of baseball is its two autonomous leagues. This is the basic structure of the game. No other sport has ever had this. Other sports have divisions and conferences, but all the teams can play each other during the regular season. Pro football is played by one league, the National Football League, but major-league baseball is the National and American Leagues. The NL and AL have distinct identities. The World Series is the greatest championship event not only because it takes a week rather than an evening of prime advertising time, but because the teams have never played each other for keeps. This is baseball's most grand and durable design. It also makes for good two league questions.

The leagues were rigidly separated by history. The NL was founded in 1876, and fought off all comers, even a rebellion by idealistic players, until 1903, when the American League, under the shrewd and tenacious leadership of Ban Johnson, signed a peace agreement that gave the AL major league status and called for a World Series. This arrangement did not keep John McGraw from refusing to play Boston in '04 for the World Championship, and for years the AL suspected that the NL would sabotage it, given the opportunity. The leagues were separate. There was no significant interleague trading until the 1960s. A player had to be waived out of one league, which meant every team in that league had a chance to claim him, before he could be dealt to the other.

This rigid separation led to some of the most enduring questions: Which league was better? Do the leagues have different styles? How would the stars in one league do in the other? It was like wondering how the characters in the Old Testament would do in the New.

Has anyone ever led the NL and AL in hitting?

For players who played their entire careers in the twentieth century, the answer is no; but the answer may be yes if one goes back to the turn of the century, when stars jumped the NL for higher salaries in the new AL. Ed Delahanty led the NL in 1899, hitting .408 for Philadelphia, and led the AL in 1902 at .376.

It's interesting that since free agency began in 1976, no one has won the batting title in both leagues.

Has anyone led both leagues in home runs?

No one who played solely in this century has led both leagues in homers, but Sam Crawford, Cobb's slugging partner, led the AL in HRs in '08, and also led the NL in '01 with 16 for the Reds. Buck Freeman, the first baseman on the first World Championship team, the '03 Boston Americans, led the AL with 13 homers. Freeman had previously led the NL by hitting 25 (thought to have been the record until reporters dug up Ned Williamson's 27 while Ruth was hitting 29 in '19) for Washington in '99.

A good but incorrect guess would be Dave Kingman, who is the answer to the best divisional question: Who is the only man to play in all four divisions in the same season? Kingman did it in '77, having played for California, the Yankees, the Mets, and the Padres. He was obstreperous enough to play for many teams in both leagues and led in homers twice, but both times in the National League.

Has anyone led both leagues in RBIs?

RBIs weren't kept as a stat until 1907,, and *TSN Record Book* doesn't record them until that year. Macmillan, in its wisdom, has calculated RBI figures going back to 1876, so Macmillan provides an undisputed answer. Since no one who played entirely in this century has been able to lead both leagues in BA or homers, if you guess Delahanty or Lajoie, you are right. Lajoie, Macmillan informs us, led the NL in 1898 with 127, and the AL in both 1901 and 1904 with 125 and 102 respectively.

Frank Robinson would be an intelligent guess, since he won the Triple Crown in the AL in '66, but great as that lean, quick-wristed slugger was in his many NL seasons, he never led in RBIs. This is a testament to how good the National League was in Robinson's prime.

Who was the first player to hit 30 home runs in each league?

This question must be approached with logic. No one hit more than 29 homers with the dead ball, so we know this happened after 1920. We also know that prior to 1960 there was no serious interleague trading, so the first 30–30 man is likely to be post expansion.

Another angle is position. A slugger who plays shortstop or third base is difficult to replace. A slugger who plays his position well is also difficult to replace. A likely position for a tradable slugger is first base, where almost anyone can play, or left field. DH, of course, collects all sorts of residue, but the first 30-and-30 man predates the DH by a decade. All this brings us to Dick Stuart, who once hit 66 home runs in the minor leagues, and whom the Pirates, in the first instance of what was to become a paradigm of the interleague trade, sent to the American League for pitching.

Stuart is arguably the worst-fielding regular first baseman of all time, and there have been some terrible ones. In the twenties and thirties, men like Zeke Bonura and Lew Fonseca set a standard for ineptitude not seen before the live ball, which began the erosion of the two-way player that climaxed with the DH. Stuart was the biggest "greaser" in that pre-Beatles time when young men were sideburned, slicked-back sons of Elvis. He claimed he wore a uniform a full size too small because "if I look bitchin', it adds 20 points to my average."

Since Stuart, seven men have hit 30 homers in each league. Name them.

Frank Robinson is obviously one. He's yet another example of the difficulty of trading for pitching. Milt Pappas didn't pitch badly in the NL, but Robinson won the Triple Crown and MVP in his first AL season and went on to be the franchise, as they say, of the next American League dynasty. At the time of the trade Cincinnati general manager Bill DeWitt said Robinson was "an old thirty." Few men have lived to regret their words as keenly as DeWitt, who earned the name "Dimwit" for the Robinson deal. Though Cincinnati had Lee May and Tony Perez in the wings, two good players don't equal one great one.

The pattern of NL muscle for AL pitching brought Frank Howard, who was the first man to hit 30 in Chavez Ravine, to Washington, where he was the first man to hit 40 for the new Senators. The Dodgers got Claude Osteen, who gave them a third starter behind Koufax and Drysdale, and won two pennants. A reversal of the pattern sent Reggie Smith to the NL for Rick Wise. Smith hit 30 once in Boston, which he said was a racist city years before that was apparent to the rest of the country, and was one of four Dodgers to hit 30 in 1977, the only time that has ever been done.

The others are Greg Luzinski, whom the Phillies sold to the White Sox; Darrell Evans, an underappreciated slugger who came to Detroit as a free agent and who hit 40 in each league; Jason Thompson; and Dave Winfield.

Minor-league questions are beyond the scope of most of our knowledge, but can provide interesting information. It's nice to know that a man named Lyman Lamb once hit 100 doubles in an organized baseball season, but beyond the novelty of the number (minor-league records are the science fiction of baseball: Joe Bauman's 72 homers in 1954 in Class C, and Bob Crues's 254 RBIs in 1948, are the outer limits of slugging), Lamb is not relevant to big-league baseball. Here is a major- and minor-league question that is relevant.

Name the last active player (he went to Japan in 1988) who had over a thousand hits in both the major and minor leagues.

This is better than Lyman Lamb or Joe Bauman, because most of us don't know enough to extrapolate an answer to a purely minor-league question. Lamb or Bauman are beyond our pale, but the recent player with a thousand major- and minor-league hits is not.

Why would a man get a thousand minor-league hits? First, he would have to be a good hitter. That isn't much of a clue, as the minors are full of good hitters, but we need to ask why a good hitter spent so much time in the minors? Perhaps he couldn't field. If he got a thousand big-league hits and couldn't field, he must have spent some time as a DH. Now we are getting somewhere. Perhaps the reason he stayed in the minors so long is that he came up with a National League team, and didn't get to be a DH until later in his career.

All this is true. The answer is Mike Easler.

Name the career home-run leaders in the American major leagues, the Japanese leagues, and the Mexican league.

This, the most interesting multi-league question, is another way of asking for the career home-run leader in the Mexican League, but phrasing is important, and putting the question in a global context makes this information less trivial. Everyone should know Henry Aaron and Sadaharu Oh, but not everyone knows Hector Espino, who played in Mexico for over 25 years, declined offers to play in the United States, and hit 484 home runs.

What was the idealists' league that the National League destroyed?

Major-league players revolted in 1890 and formed their own league. The Players League is one of the most interesting and least-known episodes in American sports history. For one year, players operated their own league in competition with the National League. They were part owners of their teams, sat on the league council, and were to share the profits.

Why did the players revolt?

The issue was salaries. The early moguls instituted the Reserve Clause, a rider on the standard player contract that bound a player to his team for a year after the contract expired. This stopped free agency, or "revolving," as it was called then, and kept salaries down. A player sued for his freedom in 1882 and a judge threw out the suit, ruling that men play baseball for "fun." The issue of whether baseball was subject to law reached the Supreme Court in 1922, and the court ruled that it was not, because, according to Justice Oliver Wendell Holmes, the professional game was "personal effort," not "commerce."

What had the owners done to precipitate the revolt?

In 1888 the owners announced a salary ceiling of $2,500 and a "Classification Plan" that ranked each player according to a scale from A to E, and paid them accordingly, with A players making $2,500 and E players drawing $500. E players would also take tickets and clean the grandstand after games.

Who led the players?

They turned to John Montgomery "Monte" Ward, a New York Giant shortstop who had a law degree from Columbia, and who had started a kind of baseball union, the Brotherhood of Professional Base Ball Players, in 1885. In 1889, Ward and the Brotherhood announced that they would run their own league in 1890.

Who led the owners?

Albert G. Spalding, the former pitcher and owner of the Chicago White Stockings, was the most powerful owner. He owned Spalding Sporting Goods, which had a virtual monopoly on sporting goods by 1890.

Rarely have two adversaries stood for such opposites. It's often said that elections in America decide very little, because Republicans and Democrats stand for the same thing, and this is the strength of our system: extremes are avoided and business can be done as usual. The Ward-Spalding confrontation, the battle of the Players League and the National League, was no such contest. It was establishment and rebellion, and the structure of American professional sports hung in the balance.

Spalding had been a player. He was the first famous pitcher, discovered when his Rockford, Illinois, team defeated the Washington Nationals, a well-known barnstorming team, in 1868. Young Spalding was acclaimed "the best pitcher in the west." The rest, as they say, is history, or, to be precise, archetype. Spalding turned professional and was the greatest pitcher in the National Association, the league that preceded the National League. His jumping to Chicago helped destroy the Association. Spalding was 46–13 in the NL's first year, and learned the business of baseball from Chicago owner William Hulbert, the man who founded the

National League. Spalding quickly made the transition to management and, after Hulbert's death, got control of the White Stockings.

There is no success story like Spalding's. He was player, owner, and captain of an industry. He was the John D. Rockefeller of the sporting world. That he was not socially prominent, a member of the ruling class, or elected to the U.S. Senate in 1910—the only thing A.G. ever failed at—does not change the fact that in his world, the world of the sports pages, he was a king.

Were Ward and Spalding evenly matched?

If Spalding did everything a man could do in baseball as a businessman, Ward did everything a man could do as a player. He started as a pitcher the year Spalding retired, 1878, won 22 games, and led the NL in ERA. He won 40 games the next two seasons and, like Spalding, pitched a perfect game.

In the early 1880s, Ward's arm went bad and he switched to shortstop, but not before compiling a 161–101 career pitching mark, and a 2.10 ERA, which is the fourth lowest of all time. He was one of the best fielding shortstops of the 1880s, and also played the outfield and third. Ward's life BA is only .278, but he hit .300 three times, once hit .369, and twice led in stolen bases. Some histories credit him with developing the raised pitching mound and perfecting the curveball. Babe Ruth is the only other top pitcher who then starred at another position.

Ward tried to improve the lot of the everyday

ballplayer. Spalding wanted to be rich and powerful. You decide whether they were evenly matched.

What did the Brotherhood do when the owners announced the Classification Plan?

The owners waited for Ward to leave the country on Spalding's 1888–89 World Tour before springing Classification on the players. The players assumed they would strike, but when Ward returned, he told them to play but not sign new contracts. After the '89 season he announced the formation of the Players League, and the stage was set for war.

The Players League was a choice, not an echo, as conservatives like to say. Players and backers owned the eight teams. There was no Reserve Clause. Eighty percent of the players chose Ward's league over Spalding's. Many invested their savings.

Has there ever been an ideological pennant race?

In 1890 the split between worker and boss, liberal and conservative, idealist and pragmatist, Populist and Republican was made flesh and put on display behind a turnstile. The players chose first. The National League, not surprisingly, gave up the salary ceiling as soon as there was competition, and tried to buy back stars. Spalding offered King Kelly, the roistering ladies' man, Boston ethnic hero, and most popular player of the 1880s, a blank check, but Kelly refused, saying he couldn't be a "traitor to the boys." The era's best fielding shortstop, Jack Glasscock, was bribed back to the NL and earned the name "Judas." Cap Anson, the man who took credit for segregating baseball, stayed in the National League.

If the Players League had the most talent, why didn't it survive?

The 1890 season unfolded like a tragedy for Ward and the Brotherhood. They won the battle for the hearts and minds of players. The next battle was strategy. The new league had to confront the issue of Sunday ball, liquor sales at games, and scheduling. The National League had been puritanical from its inception. Hulbert wouldn't play on Sunday or allow beer or liquor sales. The American Association, which started in 1882, played on Sunday and allowed liquor; the NL severely criticized its competitor for this. After Hulbert's death, Spalding kept the National League out of St. Louis because he didn't like the Sunday practices of German immigrants. Catholic immigrants thought a man should be able to enjoy himself after church, attend a baseball game, and drink beer. Monte Ward opted for respectability. The Players League did not play on Sundays or sell liquor. It also, like the NL and unlike the American Association, charged 50 cents admission, rather than a quarter. Ward seems to have copied the NL in all the ways he thought the old league was superior to the AA. Apparently he thought his league was going "first class." Scheduling was crucial. The Players announced their schedule first and Spalding scheduled NL games to conflict with as many dates as possible. His strategy

110

was clear. This war was a war of attrition. Ward refused to change the PL schedule.

What role did the media play?

A key front of the Brotherhood war was the press. Ward had cultivated editors, most notably Francis Richter of *Sporting Life*. Spalding had his newspaper allies, and later said that "printer's ink and bluff" took the place of "gunpowder and shot." A.G. bought *The New York Sporting Times* and installed the bitterly anti-Player O. P. Caylor as sports editor. Spalding never let up on the propaganda front. He called the Players "anarchists" and "terrorists," and their backers "long chance capitalists," which, of course, was exactly what he'd been when he helped Hulbert start the National League, and when he went into the sporting goods business. Ward, for his part, eloquently spoke of the experiment of men owning their own clubs, decried the tyranny of the Reserve Clause, and issued a Players' Manifesto.

Spalding's biggest ally was the dean of baseball writers, Henry Chadwick. Chadwick, though English-born, lived most of his life in New York, and had been writing about baseball since the 1840s. He constantly urged better sportsmanship, hated rowdyism and gambling, and was ferociously conservative. Chadwick saw the Players as anarchists and Al Spalding as the savior of everything he had been preaching for forty years. Chadwick had also been on Spalding's payroll for years as a contributor and editor of *Spalding's Official Base Ball Guides*. He had a flowing patrician beard and an Englishman's sense of the decent way to do things, coupled with an American appreciation for a dollar. The "Father of Base Ball," as Chadwick was called in 1890, railed against the Players all summer.

The season started well for Ward's league. Whether kranks, as fans were called, sympathized with men standing up to their bosses, or preferred better baseball, the PL outdrew the NL. The *Boston Globe* reported that when Ward and his Brooklyn Wonders came to Boston, they were mobbed at the station, where the crowd wanted to touch his coach. Though the home team was beaten ("the Brooklyn men got most of the plucky hits"), the *Globe* reported that "brotherhood . . . was in the air, and pervading every part of the grounds was a sportive kindliness and delight. . . . One man bubbled over in his glee: 'We are all in it'; and apparently that was the controlling idea."

As the season wore on, clubs lost money. The only PL club that made money was Boston, where King Kelly and the Reds went on to win the pennant. Boston had always been an ardent ball town, and the Democratic machine backed the Players. Other PL cities weren't so lucky. The PL's Philadelphia Quakers would have collapsed in July, but wealthy investors saved the team. The NL Giants had to be saved by Spalding, and Boston and Pittsburgh had to be helped. Spalding said he wanted "war to the knife," and got it. By all accounts, the NL lost more than the PL, but with Spalding and his millions, the NL had more to lose. The final attendance figures, though both sides undoubtedly inflated them, were 980,887 for the PL and 813,678 for the older league.

After the season, the Players had a moment of glory when they bought the NL Cincinnati club. Many newspapers thought the PL had won the war, but the league had been slipping away from Ward. No club made enough profit for players and backers to share, and several didn't meet their payrolls. PL backers were rumored to have met secretly with Spalding during the summer.

The weakness of Ward's league was not on the field, but in its financial structure. It's debatable how many of the backers, besides Al Johnson, the progressive Cleveland trolley magnate, believed in the league's ideals. They probably were "long chance capitalists." They certainly weren't looking to lose money. PL attendance fell as the season progressed. Kranks may have wearied of the politics of baseball. Midway through the season, Spalding used his economic muscle and threatened to withdraw advertising for Spalding products from any newspaper or magazine that carried reports of Players League games.

The Players League had too much idealism and too little capital. The league's weak link was its backers. Spalding knew that men losing money would lose their ideals, and if the backers could be alienated from the players, the league would collapse.

Is baseball a game, a dream, or a business?

The answer, of course, is all three. In 1890, athletes tried to take over the means of production of the dream and failed. They didn't have enough money to run a league. They turned to monied men, and in the end, the monied men turned on them. Fan support wasn't enough. Good baseball wasn't enough. It is interesting that after a hundred years, the pendulum has gone the other way, and fans now think players are overpaid and wither on the vine of guaranteed contracts. We still haven't resolved our ambivalence about a game, sold as entertainment, which is as necessary to our daydreams as night dreaming is to sleep.

Monte Ward stepped squarely into baseball's identity crisis. Is it a game or a business? He also rode the horns of the contradictory American attitude toward revolution. We like to believe we are free because of our Revolution, and we teach our children they're free, but free to do what? To make money, certainly. Look at Albert Spalding. But are we free to change the way money is made, so that it benefits employees as well as owners? Look at Monte Ward.

How did Spalding beat the Players?

A peace meeting was called at the Fifth Avenue Hotel in New York in October. Spalding shrewdly refused to meet with Ward or any player. He met with the backers, and that was the death knell of the Players League. A.G. later said he'd been willing to compromise, but had bluffed the backers into admitting their losses, then toughened his stance and destroyed the PL. I think this is the cherry-tree version of what happened. I suspect he had met secretly with some of them, and that cash and

under-the-table arrangements, rather than panache, did in the Players. Ward and his men sat in
the hall while, in Albert Spalding's words, "the monied men met with the monied men." These immortal words sum up most of American history.

Was Ward's experiment hamstrung by his character?

Like Spalding, Ward seems to have been obsessed
with respectability. He wouldn't let the Players play
on Sunday, sell liquor, or charge a quarter admission. He also didn't try to re-sign stars who jumped
the PL. Ward revered education and believed in the
law. Spalding rose above the law. This is the difference between them. Ward was a lawyer who told
men not to sign 1889 contracts, so that they
wouldn't be breaking the law when they left the
National League. Spalding had no such difficulty
with legality. When New York courts turned down
the NL suits to hold Giant players who played out
their Reserve time, Spalding wasn't troubled by the
fact the owners had illegally bound players to teams
and cheated them with low salaries; he took refuge
in thundering about "anarchists" and "long chance
capitalists."

Spalding was the establishment. He cloaked
himself in respectability and stood for the way business has always been done in this country. Ward,
the shortstop and outsider, tried to be Caesar's wife.
Ward refused to affiliate with the Knights of Labor
because he didn't want to be perceived as a radical.
He was a reformer, not a revolutionary. Could a

revolutionary have succeeded in 1890? Probably not, but the Players could have used the support of organized labor, just as they could have used the revenue from Sunday baseball and liquor sales.

Baseball, like America, starts after its revolution. 1890 is Year One.

Streak Questions

BASEBALL, like luck, runs in streaks. Listen to any game, and somebody will be on some kind of streak. Baseball is full of games within games, and streaks are at the heart of those inner games. Streaks show us the limits of the possible. How many games in a row can a man hit a home run? How many games has a team won in a row? Or lost? How many games has a pitcher won consecutively? Streaks are the essence of hitting. We can all remember an afternoon when no one could get us out, even if it was only with a Wiffle Ball. Players get in a "groove," teams get hot, the good and the bad seem to come consecutively.

The game is so discontinuous, and it's so hard to sustain action, that anything which happens twice is noteworthy. There is a streak record for everything: Pinky Higgins and Walt Dropo, men remembered only by their contemporaries, each got 12 consecutive hits. Dave Philley got nine pinch hits in a row. Ted Williams reached base 16 straight times. Ray Grimes drove in runs in 17 consecutive games in 1922. Streaks tell us how difficult it is to do something that might, at first glance, appear not so difficult. There are also streaks of futility. Bill Hands, a pitcher with the Cubs, once struck out 14 straight official at-bats. The most times at bat without a hit for a season is 70, by pitcher Bob Buhl, who did it playing for the Braves and Cubs in '62. The Cubs have a lock on the most futile streak of all: 81 consecutive seasons without winning the World Series.

Everyone knows who hit in the most consecutive games, but less well known streaks involve multiple-hit games. Who had three or more hits in the most consecutive games? It was done in 1976. (Answers to questions in this chapter are to be found at the end of the chapter, on page 137.)

The most famous streak, of course, is DiMaggio's hitting in 56 straight games. It's arguable whether a hitting streak is as important as a home-run total (would you rather have a guy hit in 56 straight games, or hit 56 home runs?), but what's not arguable is the way fans who like to be called purists think DiMaggio's streak is the great record.

The reasons why this record is so beloved tell us something about being a fan. First, baseball is played every day, so the spectacular gives way to the consistent over the life of the season, and Joe hit in 56 straight games. That was more than one-third of the 154-game season, and there are people who think that this kind of consistency defines baseball excellence. Something done every day has to be done every day. The pressure of a streak is greater than the pressure to amass a season statis-

tic. DiMaggio's streak started on May 15, 1941, and
didn't end until July 17. Unlike Pete Rose's 44-game
streak, this one had a bearing on the pennant race.
The Yankees were 17–17 when it started, but were
solidly in first place when it ended. Joe hit 15 home
runs during his streak. No one else on a hitting
streak has come close to that figure.

The mark sanctifies DiMaggio. It's important
that a great player have a record or a number to
remember him by. It serves the same purpose as a
colorful nickname. It's hard to believe Larry Berra
would have gained the notoriety and the distinction
of being what Bill James called "a walking comic
book" that Yogi did. Dizzy sounds like he throws
harder than Jay, and Babe is certainly going to hit
more home runs than George Herman. Like the ep-
ithets that Homer gave the heroes of the *Iliad,* we
need a tag or a record or, better, a number. Joe
DiMaggio, 56; Babe Ruth, 60; Ty Cobb, .367; Ted
Williams, .406. In baseball, numbers speak louder
than words. Each player who made people think he
was the greatest player they ever saw needs his
number. Willie Mays is the only one I can think of
who has a catch that reverberates like one of those
grand numbers. Joseph Paul DiMaggio needs to be
sanctified, and the hitting streak does it.

What's not as well known is that DiMaggio hit
in 61 straight games in the minors. This is not the
longest organized-baseball hitting streak. That
honor, according to Vern Luse, SABR minor-league
researcher, belongs to Daniel Stearns, who hit in 69
straight for the Topeka Golden Giants in 1887.
Walks counted as hits then, even in Topeka, so

there's no way to know if Stearns did hit in 69 games. Joe Wilhoit of Wichita hit in 69 straight games in 1919. DiMaggio's minor-league streak is interesting because it adumbrates his major-league streak.

Joe had a penchant for streaks. It's also not well known that after the 56, he went on another streak of 16 games. Consistency was in his blood. That, apparently, is what those fans believe who I can't get to admit Willie Mays was better. (How could someone be a better center fielder than Willie Mays?) He did everything so easily. Apparently Joe DiMaggio played the game in a state of grace that transcends argument. It doesn't matter that Mays was faster, or had a better arm. Joe was Joe, and those who chronicled their wasted time with him feel they saw the miraculous, and achieved the peace that passeth understanding.

Who stopped Joe D's major-league hitting streak is well known, but who stopped the minor-league streak is not. This is an interesting question, or rather answer, but it requires a hint. The 56-game streak was stopped by two Cleveland pitchers, one of whom was the son of a better American League pitcher. The man who stopped the 61-game streak was also the son of an American League pitcher, and his father, whose name he bore, is in the Hall of Fame. Now memory can churn over impressions and snippets of fact, and try to recall the list of men who had the misfortune to have fathers who were better than they were. We all may suspect our fathers of being better than we are, but most of us are spared having the difference leap off the neat pages of *The Baseball Encyclopedia*. Anyone who makes the big leagues has known triumph, but these unfortunates always had the lingering question, "Am I as good as he is?" and in both these cases, the answer is a resounding no.

Most of us know that Jim Bagby, Jr., and Al Smith (along with some hot leather from third baseman Ken Keltner) stopped Joe DiMaggio on a sweltering night in Cleveland. Bagby *fils* will be remembered longer than Bagby *père* (like Tracy Stallard, linked forever to the day a boundary of greatness was set), even though Bagby senior won 30 games for the World Champion Indians of 1920. (I know the Black Sox were throwing games in September and the Cleveland pennant is tainted like the Reds' championship, but Bagby the elder still was 31–12 with the *live* ball. Only four men have won 30 games with the live ball, but Jim Bagby, Sr., just isn't remembered.)

The man who stopped DiMaggio after 61 games was Ed Walsh, Jr., son of the spitmaster and one-time winner of 40 games. The younger Walsh (one wonders if he was ever called Little Ed) had a career record of 11–24 over four lackluster years with his father's team, the White Sox. In 1933 the younger Walsh was on the way down, having accumulated that mediocre record, attended Notre Dame University, and, no doubt, more than once comtemplated the distance between his own accomplishments and his father's.

Who stopped DiMaggio's streaks is a good question, provided both streaks are mentioned, and given the odd fact that sons of more famous fathers were involved. Who stopped Pete Rose in his 1978 bid to be Joe DiMaggio? I was glad when it happened. Pete accumulated numbers, and likes to compare himself to men greater than he. It started when he passed Frankie Frisch for the most career hits by a switch-hitter, and called himself the greatest switch-hitter of all time. Mickey Mantle gets my vote. Then Pete went on the hitting streak. It was a great streak, there's no denying it. Only six men have had streaks of 40 or more games. Naming them isn't easy. There's Rose and DiMaggio, of course, and if you remember '78, you know that Rose tied Wee Willie Keeler at 44, and had passed Cobb at 40 games and George Sisler at 41. (To show the arbitrary nature of streaks, Keeler actually hit in 45 games, but number one was the last game of the 1896 season, and isn't counted, which I suppose just adds to the aesthetic aspect of streak hitting. It's a game within a game, and a streak is only a streak if everyone agrees on it.) The only other man to reach 40 was Bad Bill Dahlen of the Chicago Colts in 1894, when the league hit .309 and Philadelphia hit .349. Dahlen hit in 42 games.

Pete's streak was monumental, but thank God he got no closer to DiMaggio. It's bad enough that Rose was compared to Cobb in '85, when Pete got the hit record, but at least there are some similarities if you don't look closely. Cobb didn't hit home runs. (Of course not, because the game was different. Cobb led the AL in home runs once and in slugging eight times, including six times in a row; Pete never led in either.) They both ran the bases hard (the most stolen bases Pete ever had was 20;

Cobb stole over 50 eight times). There is no similarity between Pete and Joe DiMaggio in playing style, talent, or impact, except, of course, the hitting streaks. This seems to be Pete's genius. He parlayed above-average talent and superhuman drive into getting his name associated with the all-time greats.

Two men stopped Pete's streak. One was a rookie and one a wily veteran. The rookie was Larry McWilliams, a hard-throwing lefty. The veteran, the man who got Pete on his last at-bat, was Gene Garber, who got 25 saves that year, pitching for the Phillies and Braves. Rose was mad that Garber didn't give him a fastball his last time up, and Garber, with one of those remarks that knock on the door of immortality, said he was paid to get people out, not throw fastballs. Roger Maris was more stoic about his check-swing at Hoyt Wilhelm's knuckleball.

There's some history on Pete's side. (There's always history on Pete's side.) During DiMaggio's streak, Joe twice came to the plate hitless in the ninth, and the string could have ended with a base on balls. In game 36, Joe was 0 for 3 when he batted the last time. The Browns' pitcher Bob Moncrief pitched to DiMaggio, and Joe singled. After the game, Moncrief said he couldn't have walked him because "it wouldn't have been fair to him or me." I thought that sort of chivalry died in the First World War, but one has to admire Moncrief. In game 38, also against the Browns, Joe went into the ninth hitless and was the fourth man up. With a man on second and two out, Browns manager Joe Sewell ordered side-armer Eldon Aucker to pitch to Joe, and DiMaggio doubled. Maybe the world was more sporting then, or maybe those gentlemen wanted to be part of history, linked forever with the man they thought was the best they had seen.

Another streak is tainted. Don Drysdale's 58 scoreless innings should have ended when he hit Dick Dietz with the bases loaded, but umpire Harry Wendlstedt said Dietz didn't try to get out of the way of the pitch and refused to award him first base. Drysdale subsequently got Dietz, and the streak continued. I remember that streak, or, to be more precise, I can't forget it, because Robert Kennedy was killed during it, and the only candidate who could have ended the Vietnam War before the '72 election was dead. Perhaps I unfairly associate Drysdale with Nixon, but there is a subjective element to memory.

It's interesting that an umpire would want to make rather than adjudicate history. It happened again in 1988, when umpire Paul Runge saved Oral Hershiser's record-breaking streak by calling runner's interference on a run-scoring double play. This isn't exactly fair since umpires have such direct bearing on the game, but apparently Wendlstedt and Runge thought they were editing, not just witnessing, history. We all excuse umpires' mistakes. Look at Don Denkinger's infamous call in the '85 World Series, when he ruled Jorge Orta safe in the ninth inning of the sixth game. That's part of the game, part of what makes it like life; but umpires' mistakes have to be mistakes, errors of judgment, not willful decisions to preserve "history." Part of the game's charm is that the umpire, like the

Pope, is infallible, but, like the Pope, also human. I think Wendlstedt and Runge overstepped the bounds of charm, and I think Walter Johnson's 56 scoreless innings should be considered the record.

The record for leading a league in singles for consecutive seasons is seven, and was done in the 1950s. Who led the AL in this category for seven straight years?

Here's an interesting question: What two pitchers gave up a home run to Babe Ruth in 1927, during the march to 60, and a hit to Joe DiMaggio during the 56-game streak? This question connects two great feats and two different eras. There was a pitcher, I'm happy to say, who faced both Babe Ruth and Mickey Mantle, which is a marvelous piece of information, because, as George Orwell pointed out, we tend to think of history as a "long scroll with thick black lines ruled across it," like the "time lines" in elementary school classrooms. It's hard, though delightful, to imagine one man, Al Benton, bridging the gap between Babe Ruth and the Roaring Twenties, and Mickey Mantle and the Fabulous Fifties; but, as Orwell says, "Each age lives on into the next . . . there are innumerable human lives spanning every gap." Many fans saw the two men; Benton pitched to them. One of the joys of baseball is that by middle age, a fan has a God's-eye view. For sheer majesty of era-spanning and witnessing the turning of the generations, what compares to Ted Williams hitting a home run off

127

Thornton Lee in 1940, and then hitting a home run off his son Don in 1960?

Who could have surrendered one of the sixty and prolonged Joe D's streak? This question calls for a review of one's mental software. It has to be men who pitched a long time, and that's a good clue, because the mediocre and obscure don't last fourteen years. The answer is not, by the way, a pair of unknowns who appeared in 1927, went to the minors, and then, somewhat like Woody Allen's Zelig, reappeared in 1941 as old unknowns. These men pitched all the way from the Bull Market through the Depression, to the battle of Stalingrad.

The record for hitting 30 or more home runs in consecutive seasons is 12, and was not set by Babe Ruth. Who did it?

The men who span the ages of Ruth and DiMaggio are Lefty Grove and Ted Lyons. Grove's presence in the big leagues the summer before Pearl Harbor is a testament to the power of numbers. Lefty had long since lost his fastball (which may have been the best of all time; there is no more impressive stat than Grove's five consecutive ERAs under 3.00 from 1928 through 1932, especially his 2.54 in the jackrabbit year, 1930). Speaking of streaks, Grove led the American League in strikeouts his first seven seasons. He also won nine ERA crowns, but they weren't consecutive. Grove was such a fine pitcher that he still won ERA championships after his extraordinary fastball deserted him and he was a "stuff" pitcher in Fenway Park. Grove was pitch-

128

ing that last summer before World War II because he wanted to win 300 games. Ted Lyons, who was the same age as Grove and is also in the Hall of Fame, pitched twenty-one years with the same team, the White Sox, and never got to the World Series.

Nineteen forty-one saw the death of the man who has the most beloved streak. Lou Gehrig died on June 2, during DiMaggio's streak. The Yankees erected a plaque to his memory on July 6, and DiMaggio was still on the streak. The most interesting question about Gehrig's streak, the amazing 2,130 games played (Lou only pinch-hit in some, but the total is still remarkable), is why it is such a cherished record. Like the 60 and the 56 straight, it is an immortal number. For one thing, it canonizes a man who, as a good son and good sport, needed canonization. Nothing evokes sentimentality like an athlete dying young, as a bisexual English poet once said, and Lou Gehrig was the epitome of what an athlete was supposed to be, as opposed to the self-centered, whore-chasing, overgrown boys they usually are. No athletic figure of the century evokes so much sentimentality.

Gehrig's streak is a matter of the record fitting the man so perfectly that no one should ever be allowed to break it. Lou Gehrig was the Iron Horse. He was a model of the hardworking immigrant's son: stolid, dependable, unimaginative, dutiful, and even rescued from his mother's house by a woman who loved him. He also received American immortality when he was played by Gary Cooper in a movie and portrayed as silent strength: a bat-swing-ing Hemingway strongman, quiet, caring, good in the clutch (Gehrig did hit a record 23 grand-slam home runs—any homer record held by someone other than Babe Ruth is impressive), the very embodiment of a man too good to die.

Consistency is harder to achieve than it might appear. In the five years between 1982 and 1986, only five pitchers won at least 12 games every year. Name them.

There was another side to Gehrig that his death rectified. He was always in someone's shadow. First it was Ruth, then DiMaggio. On the day Lou hit four homers in a game (something the Babe never did), John McGraw retired and got the New York headlines. Gehrig had a genius for getting upstaged— maybe that's the fate of momma's boys and nice guys—then he got the disease and no one could upstage him. No one upstages death. His farewell at Yankee Stadium is one of the great schlock moments of all time, except that the man was really dying. It wasn't a movie. Seventy thousand New Yorkers cried, and when New Yorkers cry, it's remembered. Lou Gehrig's "I'm the luckiest man on the face of the earth" is practically an athlete's Gettysburg Address. It makes Douglas MacArthur's "Old soldiers never die" sound like the posturing of a vain jackass who's fallen out of favor.

I suspect that Gehrig's stolid dependability covered a deep resentment of Babe Ruth. They weren't Patroclus and Achilles. Ruth did everything Momma Gehrig succeeded in keeping Lou from doing. Who knows how Lou felt about that? There's a story that when Gehrig was a rookie, Ruth sent a woman into his room to help him break into big-league night life, and Gehrig sent her away. One wonders how amusing Gehrig found that. Besides the obvious showboating generosity, the Babe was pricking Gehrig's Achilles' heel. Later they didn't speak because Momma Gehrig made a remark at a Yankee picnic about Babe's adopted daughter not being as well dressed as his natural daughter. Ruth didn't speak to Gehrig until he learned Lou was dying. I suspect that incident was the tip of the massive resentment and unease they felt toward each other. One can also see Lou's side. He was awfully good to have to be in a great man's shadow.

Gehrig's consecutive-game streak may have been his quiet way of outdoing Babe Ruth. What record couldn't Babe Ruth break? A record that required dependability and going to bed at a decent hour. It should be pointed out that Ruth played over 150 games in 6 of the 16 seasons he was an outfielder, but Gehrig did it 12 times. There was, after all, something Lou Gehrig did twice as well as Babe Ruth.

Gehrig's streak is a great streak. Streaks touch something that goes back to childhood: "Let's see you do that again!" "How many in a row can you get?" They touch something primitive. Life itself runs in streaks—hot streaks, ruts, luck. We've all had the sensation things were going great and there was no explanation for it. Look at Dale Long in 1956. The heavyset journeyman first baseman hit home runs in eight consecutive games. Long was playing in Forbes Field, hardly a sluggers' paradise, and for a Kiner-less Pirate team that came in seventh. There's no explanation for it. Neither Ruth nor Gehrig nor Aaron, nor anyone until Don Mattingly in 1987, had hit home runs in eight consecutive games. It was as if the gods had intervened for Dale Long. He had never done anything like it, and he never did anything like it again. The streak didn't effect the pennant race or change Long's career. It just happened. The greatest winning streak of all time seems to be just as much an inadvertent intervention of the baseball gods. The 1916 New York Giants, managed by the irascible McGraw, won 26 games in a row. That is an astonishing figure. The 1916 Giants boasted no Hall of Famers and finished fourth, seven games out. It's hard to imagine a team winning 26 consecutive games, and harder to imagine that such a streak wouldn't put a team higher than fourth, but this is the nature of streaks. Like Dale Long's, they appear like lightning and are gone.

There's just no explanation for the '16 Giants —no aging stars overcoming career-long shortcomings, no rookie sensations whose careers would be cut tragically short, no troika of unbeatable pitchers —just a sixth-place team that got hotter than any team in modern baseball history. The Boston Red Stockings won 26 in a row in 1875, but that team was 71–8 for the season, so the competitive balance of the National Association, the first openly professional league, is suspect.

Pitchers have streaks. Tom Seaver once fanned

ten San Diego Padres in a row on an April day in 1970. This is remarkable considering that no one, not even in the nineteenth century, had ever struck out more than nine in a row. The most Nolan Ryan ever had was eight, and he did that twice. Koufax never fanned more than five consecutively.

Most fans know that Rube Marquard holds the consecutive-win record with 19, and many know that under today's scoring rules Marquard would have won 20 in a row. Like Keeler's 44, this is a matter of judgment. Carl Hubbell won 24 in a row over two seasons, but this isn't how streaks are figured. No one before 1900 ever won 20 in a row in a season, the best old-time mark also being 19, by Tim Keefe, Monte Ward's onetime brother-in-law. Interestingly, the largest number of consecutive losses is also 19, which has been done twice: by Bob Groom in 1909, and Jack Nabors in 1916. The symmetry of the winning and losing streaks is less predictable than it might appear. Losing games in large numbers is more difficult because a manager has to permit it. No one in this century has lost 30 games —the record is 29, by Vic Willis with the Boston Braves in 1905. Thirty games have been *won* 21 times.

More attention should be paid to pitchers' winning streaks. Since 1945, only seven men have won 15 or more in a row. The man with the longest post-'45 streak also has the best season won-and-lost percentage of all time for 15 or more decisions. He is the Roger Maris of relief pitchers. Elroy Face, godfather of the split-fingered fastball, then called a "forkball," won 17 straight games in 1959 and had an 18–1 record. Interestingly, Face had only ten saves.

Ewell Blackwell, once described as "a fishing pole with ears," won 16 in a row in '47, when he had one of the most overpowering years of the decade. Arm trouble kept the "Whip" from ever having a great season again. Jack Sanford won 16 straight for the pennant-bound Giants in '62: this was a case of a good pitcher having his best year for a team having its best year. Bob Gibson won 15 in a row for the Cardinals in '68, when he did everything: 1.12 ERA (lowest in the live-ball era, and fourth lowest of all time), 13 shutouts (which is the most with the live ball), and set the single-game strikeout record in the World Series by fanning 17 Tigers.

The other NL 15-game winning streak was by Steve Carlton in his amazing 1972 season. Pitching streaks depend on more than how a man pitches. His team must win, and the team can carry him on a mediocre day, or ruin him on a good day. Dave McNally won 15 straight for the powerhouse '69 Orioles, and his teammates called him "McLucky" for the kind of support he received. Carlton's streak, and his entire season, cannot be attributed to his team. The '72 Phillies were awful. They won 59 games; only San Diego won fewer, with 58. They batted .236 and scored the fewest runs in the league. Steve Carlton won 27 of those 59 games. A pitcher may never have had a better year. Twenty-seven was the most Sandy Koufax ever won, and he did it with a pennant winner. Carlton had a 1.97 ERA and struck out 310 batters in 346 innings. He won pitching's triple crown, leading in wins, ERA, and strikeouts. Add the 15-game winning streak to that season, and it boggles the mind that anyone could do it, let alone for a last-place club.

The other 15-game streak belongs to Gaylord Perry in '74. Perry, like Carlton, had been traded for an inferior pitcher in '72: Carlton for Rick Wise and Perry for Sam McDowell, and both Carlton and Perry became better pitchers. In '72, Gaylord won 24 and lost 16. His ERA was 1.92. The Indians came in second to last. This is a normal great year with a bad team. Carlton's '72 season is simply off the scale of greatness.

What is the record for scoring runs in consecutive games in the twentieth century? Who holds it and when was it done?

Streaks appeal to the imagination because they are aesthetic rather than practical. Their value lies in the intangible world of luck and fate. Cal Ripken had the most idiosyncratic streak. He played 8,243 consecutive innings. Why? There was no rational reason. Did Ripkin want a record? SABR researcher Ray Gonzalez discovered that Gehrig played every inning of every game only in 1931, so Ripken easily played the most consecutive innings. What a strange compulsion! Everyone from Oriole management to Baltimore talk-show callers thought he'd play better and hit more if he got some rest, but the man wanted to play every second of every game. Was it a superstition? Ballplayers are as superstitious as primitive tribesmen, and why not? The laws of their world and the gods who rule it are as mysterious and capricious as any facing a bushman. Perhaps Ripken felt his career was a streak. Someone should study the psychopathology of the daily life of ballplayers.

It's been said that baseball is a rational game that mirrors the vision the Founding Fathers had of America. The game has rules; it has checks and balances whereby one man can't dominate the whole season; a team is a collection of individuals, not a gang; and so on. Baseball is a rational game, except that the men who have played it, since its inception, have been as superstitious as witch doctors, and the history of baseball shibboleths, good-luck charms, rituals, talismans, pre-game diets, and all the odd, fate-supplicating behavior in which players have indulged through the years, would fill an encyclopedia. For three years a man named Charles Victory Faust warmed up for the Giants before every game, even though he wasn't under contract, because McGraw thought he brought luck. How many players haven't changed their underwear after getting two hits, or not signed their names the day they pitched, or avoided the white lines when coming in from the field during a game? Wade Boggs eats only chicken before he plays; his wife has been required to find as many ways of preparing fowl as Boggs has of adjusting to the curveball.

What's so marvelous about this symmetrical game, which does mirror an Enlightment vision of well-governed citizens, is that those who play it immerse themselves in every imaginable ritual and superstition. This is a testament to how difficult the game is to play.

The Answer Is Baseball

Baseball, of course, is a matter of everyday performance, not of sporadic heroics, but fans love streaks. In 1987 Paul Molitor hit in 39 straight games, which is the seventh longest streak of all time. The night he was stopped, fans booed when the winning run scored in the tenth inning with a hitless Molitor on deck. The crowd wanted the runner to stop at third so Molitor would have another at-bat. This shows such a clear preference for aesthetics over winning that one has to smile.

Answers to questions in the preceding chapter:

- The player who had three or more hits in the most consecutive games was George Brett, with six games in 1976.

- It was Nellie Fox, who recently came so close to being elected to the Hall of Fame, who led the AL in singles for seven years.

- Jimmie Foxx, who had no trouble being elected to the Hall, holds the record for hitting 30 or more home runs in consecutive seasons.

- Between 1982 and 1986, the five pitchers to win at least twelve games each per season were Jack Morris, Fernando Valenzuela, John Tudor, Bill Gullickson, and Charlie Hough.

- The twentieth-century record for runs scored in consecutive games is held by Red Rolfe with 18 in 1930.

137

The Riddle of the Indian

TOWARD the end of the decade that started with the players' revolt, saw the mound moved back to 60 feet 6 inches, and witnessed the consolidation of major-league baseball into the "big league"—the expression signified the National League monopoly, not the league's status—a small drama was played out that still haunts the collective fan imagination: the rise and fall of the first man known to be Indian who played major-league baseball.

Who was the first big-league Indian?

In fact, the first was James Madison Toy, who played in the American Association in 1887 and 1890, but this is a discovery of research. The first man known and treated as Indian was Louis Sockalexis—a name that intrigued sportswriters in 1897, who thought it befitted a slugger. Sockalexis was a Penobscot born in Old Town, Maine, in 1871, the year of birth of Marcel Proust and the National Association. He was not full-blooded (the last full-blooded Penobscot died in 1853), and he was not,

141

as the papers in 1897 liked to say, the son of the chief. The tribe did not have a chief in 1871.

There are only a few details about this man who John McGraw and Hughie Jennings said was the finest natural talent they ever saw that seem to be reliable. The *Encyclopedia* says Louis Sockalexis played 66 games in '97 and hit .338, 21 games in '98 and hit .224, and 7 games in '99 and hit .273, which gives this early Native American a .313 life BA, achieved in 94 games with 367 at-bats, which isn't even a full season. None of his numbers are particularly impressive, but this man's story is anything but dull.

The *Encyclopedia* gives us the bones of Sockalexis's life. He was born on October 24, 1871, died on Christmas Eve, 1913, was called "Chief," played a fraction of three seasons, and occupies about the same space on his page in Macmillan's book of books as does Redleg Snyder, an anonymous nineteenth-century ballplayer who played fewer games than Sockalexis. The Indian's three lines are more than Moe Solomon, a few entries below, who, the book tells us, was called the "Rabbi of Swat," and who, I once learned from a SABR publication and Bill James's *Historical Abstract,* had the misfortune to be the first highly touted Jewish prospect signed by a New York club. Amid tremendous fanfare, Solomon was brought to the major leagues too quickly and was a two-game bust.

Ethnicity is crucial to baseball. Here the game jumps its self-contained perfection, its numbers and patterns, and enters the national imagination. Every group has been represented and every group has a story. Solomon wasn't the first Jewish player. Henry Adams called the Jews "eternal contemporaries," and baseball is no exception. Lipman Pike, a Jewish New Yorker, played in the National Association in each year of its existence, and batted .321. Pike played for St. Louis in the National League's first season, and was a part-time player in three more. He also managed in the Association for two years and for a year in the NL. His brother Jay appeared in one game in 1877. Levi Meyerle, who the *Encyclopedia* tells us was called "Long Levi," played in the National Association and pitched two games for Philadelphia in '76. Meyerle was thought to be Jewish, though he denied it. Johnny Kling, the great defensive catcher for the '06 Cubs, the club that won 116 out of 154 games (38 losses!), has been reported to be Jewish. Nothing was said about it while he played, so Kling, like the boxer Max Baer, may not have been Jewish. The all-time great Jewish catcher is Moe Berg, who was the most interesting person who ever played, having been a scholar and a spy as well as a catcher. Berg may be the only baseball player to contemplate assassinating a nuclear scientist, as he did in 1944, when he attended a convention in Switzerland with Werner Heisenberg. Berg decided the Germans weren't close to developing the atomic bomb, and the Nazi physicist was spared.

Baseball has been a great psychological melting pot. The Irish played the game in the 1890s, then came the Germans, Poles, Italians, Hispanics, and finally blacks. The effect on the psyche of the country, not to mention the effect on each group, was

143

enormous. Philip Roth, in a terrific piece titled "My Baseball Years," said that "for someone whose roots in America were strong but only inches deep . . . baseball was a kind of secular church that reached into every class and region of the nation . . . baseball made me understand patriotism at its best." Baseball has been a visible symbol of the best in America for many of us. Racists had every reason to fear Jackie Robinson, for the arena of baseball is the national imagination, and if the black man could play there, sooner or later he could play anywhere. It's not surprising that Robinson broke the twentieth-century color bar seven years before the Supreme Court ordered school integration.

Who was the first player of Polish ancestry? (Answers to this and subsequent questions in this chapter are to be found at the end of the chapter, on page 160.)

The first Indian was another matter. The Indian strikes a different psychic chord from that struck by the black man, and no one tried to exclude him from baseball. It's been many years since a forest full of Indians troubled the American mind. We slaughtered them and devastated their cultures so completely that we've even eradicated our guilt about it. Indians represent a past we want to remember: the struggle to settle the country, subdue nature, and conquer the frontier. The black man is from a past that is not so easy to romanticize, and a present we can't ignore. The Indian hasn't been a

144

sexual threat since the novels of James Fenimore Cooper.

Sockalexis appeared four years after a distinct turning point in the American self-image. In 1893, an unknown history professor named Frederick Jackson Turner pointed out that since publication of the 1890 census, the United States no longer had a frontier. In the most famous academic paper ever presented in America, Turner asked a question that still haunts our conceptions of ourselves: What would happen to the American character without the experience of the frontier? Turner postulated that the country's whole learning of democracy was a result of the frontier experience. When one thinks of how bustling and mercantile America was by the 1890s, his question almost becomes a lament. The economy had become industrialized. Big cities like New York and Chicago were really big, and their slums were teeming. As farmers found out with the Populist Party, power in this country was in Wall Street and the smoky rooms where "monied men" and politicians did business.

By the 1890s it was obvious that power did not lie in yeoman farmers, each occupying his own tract of land, as Thomas Jefferson had predicted and hoped. Power lay, as Jefferson's antagonist, Alexander Hamilton, said it would, in the banking system of a manufacturing nation. These two thinkers, prophets, and intellectual adversaries, like Ward and Spalding, saw America as two different places. Jefferson, a plantation owner from a state without large cities, saw land and the political potential of men owning land. Hamilton, the illegitimate son of

a British merchant in the West Indies, came to co-
lonial Manhattan and saw the economic potential of
cities.

Why is this important? Why is Sockalexis important? The answer to both questions begins with
another question: How and why did baseball become so deeply rooted in the American psyche?
Baseball took hold of our imagination during the
post—Civil War boom that transformed America
from a rural, agricultural country, concerned with
settling a vast wilderness, to an industrial giant
ready to take on the world.

It is against this background of a country that
liked to think itself the Jeffersonian "last best hope
of mankind," but was being forced to realize it was
really Hamilton's paradise for bankers, that baseball
becomes the national pastime. It is into this booming, mercantile place learning to live in cities, but
cherishing a revolutionary past and a vanished frontier, that, in 1897, an Indian appears for the Cleveland Spiders. An obscure history professor makes
himself famous by asking rhetorical questions about
the frontier, but avoids mentioning Indians or other
frontier elements in the American character, like
the rootin'-tootin'-shoot-'em-up-Yahoo mentality
that creeps into our actions every so often, and
what should appear on the green fields of the national pastime but an Indian? Against the background of a lamented frontier and lamented
American opportunity comes a national game
played on green fields in big cities for money, and
an Indian appears who may be able to play the game

on the green dream frontier better than anyone who has ever played it. This is an interesting story.

The first player of Italian ancestry was Eddie Abbaticchio, who played for nine years. Within five years, in what year did this gentleman broaden the national ethnic consciousness?

Sockalexis was an immediate sensation. Fans got news through newspapers and by word of mouth. There were no newsreels and no action photos in newspapers. It was a pre-visual culture. Expectations were built with adjectives. Great feats were reported, and fans had to imagine the home run, the slide, or throw. Reading the Boston papers for April 1897, one gets a sense of something happening, something building, a hero out there in the West—reports from St. Louis, Louisville, Cleveland. *Sporting Life,* a weekly baseball bible and competitor of *The Sporting News,* reported that in six exhibition games in April, Sockalexis had ten outfield assists. That's enough to fire anyone's imagination. When the season started, "Sock," as the papers called him, made a great catch with the bases loaded at Robison Field against the Cardinals in St. Louis to save a game. A few days later he made a tremendous throw in Louisville. Sockalexis was five feet eleven and weighed 190 pounds, which, given the height of the average man in 1897, would be like being six-three or six-four and weighing 230 pounds today. He was as big as a football lineman of his day, and faster than the backs. Sockalexis re-

putedly had run a hundred yards, in a baseball uniform, in ten seconds flat, which was close to the
world record.

There is nothing as exciting as the arrival of a
superstar. Look at the anticipation that surrounded
Jose Canseco in 1986. The Oakland slugger hit 33
home runs, so all that publicity and rising rookie
card prices weren't a noose around his neck.
Mickey Mantle was given number 6 when he arrived
in New York, to follow Ruth's 3, Gehrig's 4, and
DiMaggio's 5. Mantle required a little more season-
ing, and when he returned from the minors, he got
number 7. A new star raises the level of the game.
There's always the possibility that he may, in fact,
be the best we've seen—a man to chronicle our
wasted time and make us feel like groundlings at
the Globe, rather than devotees of soap operas. Before fans saw Sockalexis, they heard about him, and
created their own image of a man who could throw
out ten runners from the outfield in six pre-season
games, or run a hundred yards as fast as anyone on
earth. Anticipation is often sweeter than reality. It
is its own excitement, but anticipation makes de-
mands and extracts a price. Anticipation of Sockalexis must have been feverish.

When Sockalexis came to Boston to play the
National League team that once called itself the Red
Stockings, and was then known as the Beaneaters,
he was not a stranger. He played baseball at Holy
Cross in '95 and '96, and had been a sensation.
College baseball was more important in the 1890s
than in this century. Colleges recruited for baseball
then the way they do now for football. The best

teams in the country were Brown University in Providence, and Holy Cross in Worcester, Massachusetts. When these two powers met in 1895, and Sockalexis stole six bases to lead the Crusaders to a 13–4 victory, there were five future big-leaguers playing for HC, and two for Brown.

Sockalexis got to Holy Cross, like a young hero in a legend, because of a tutelary figure, Mike "Doc" Powers. Powers was the Holy Cross baseball captain, and discovered Sockalexis while barnstorming in Maine during the summer of '94. Sockalexis was also seen in Maine by Gilbert Patten, who, under the name of Burt L. Standish, became the most prolific writer of children's baseball novels. The Indian may have been the inspiration for Patten's character Frank Merriwell.

Doc Powers was a charismatic man, a year older than Sockalexis. Powers was studying to be a doctor. He later caught for the Philadelphia A's and was an excellent defensive backstop and signal caller, but not much of a hitter. Powers was Eddie Plank's favorite receiver, and like Sockalexis, his career was cut tragically short. Doc Powers caught the first game played at Shibe Park in 1909, and ran into a railing while chasing a foul ball. Two weeks later he died of gangrene of the intestine.

After Holy Cross, Sockalexis followed Powers to Notre Dame, where Doc was baseball captain, but Sockalexis only stayed for a month before joining the Cleveland club. The Indian didn't choose Cleveland because of the name of the team, which didn't become Indians until 1915. They were the Cleveland Spiders, which has to be one of the oddest names a major-league team has ever had. In 1889 one of the owners remarked that the players were "skinny as spiders," and the name stuck. The exoticness of nineteenth-century player nicknames has been well documented ("Chicken" Wolf, "The Only" Nolan, Bob "Death to Flying Things" Ferguson, "Trick" McSorley, "Icebox" Chamberlain, etc.), but teams also had names that strike the modern ear as strange—the Pittsburgh Innocents, the Brooklyn Bridegrooms (one year a number of the players got married), the Elizabeth Resolutes, and the Troy Haymakers. (The Haymakers' name was used by Robert Coover in his wonderful novel about the psychology of a baseball nut, *The Universal Baseball Association, Inc., J. Henry Waugh, Prop.*) Cleveland seems to have had a run of unusual names. The Association team was the Forest Cities, which is explainable inasmuch as Cleveland had long been known as the Forest City, but then Spiders, Exiles (the team was so unpopular in 1899 because of the syndicate system, which put Cleveland's best men in St. Louis—the Robison brothers owned both the Cleveland and St. Louis franchises —that the Spiders finished the season playing only away games), Bronchos, Blues, Naps (after Napoleon Lajoie, great player and manager), Molly Maguires, and finally, in 1915, in response to a contest, fans gave the team the official nickname "Indians" in memory of Sockalexis, which makes the Indians the only current team named after a player. In the last century and the early years of this one, clubs were most frequently referred to by city and league,

like Boston Nationals or New York Americans. Many
of the nicknames that seem as natural to our ears
as "we hold these truths to be self-evident," like
Yankees and Cubs, were actually the coinages of
sportswriters.

*No less than four of the consensus All-Time team
are of one non-Anglo-Saxon ethnic group. Name
the group and those players.*

Sockalexis went to Cleveland because of Jesse Bur-
kett, the .400-hitting Hall of Fame outfielder, who
coached at Holy Cross during the winters of '94 and
'95. In the 1890s it was common for a professional
player to coach a college team during the winter.
When the coach left for spring training, which in
the '90s usually meant spring drying out, the college
nine would be run by its captain and a manager,
who was frequently a student. It wasn't until the
second decade of the twentieth century that colleges got full-time baseball coaches.

Sockalexis started hot. At the end of his first
week, he was hitting .375. He hit a home run over
the centerfield fence in St. Louis on April 30, and a
bases-loaded triple the next day. In a game on May
3, *Sporting Life* reported that "derisive ki-yi's" from
the stands didn't bother him. The next day the Indian homered, two days later he tripled, and two
days after that he went on an extra-base-hit tear,
hitting three doubles and two triples, and stealing
three bases in four games, all the while playing a

magnificent right field. On May 17, *Sporting Life* says 17,000 fans came out to see him at Washington Park in Brooklyn, even though the first game of a doubleheader was rained out. At the end of May, he was hitting .360.

The Indian's fortunes in that brief season are a parabola. They start with the exhibition buildup, then big crowds, "ki-yi's" and war whoops, fine play, more crowds, more expectation, and then— what was to be the high point of his career—his first trip to New York in June. Sockalexis had been in Brooklyn, but Brooklyn wasn't New York. Brooklyn was a separate city until 1898, when Chicago threatened to grow bigger, and Brooklyn was annexed to keep Gotham the biggest city in America. New York then, as now, was the media and cultural capital. The appearance of a new star did not go unheeded. The Giants' best pitcher was Amos Rusie, the Hoosier Thunderbolt, who had come roaring back after holding out the entire '96 season. The New York papers made much of the confrontation between the hardest thrower of the decade and the Indian from Maine.

What little literature there is on Sockalexis never fails to mention the confrontation with Rusie. Some accounts claim the muscular Indian hit a 600-foot home run off Rusie, which would be a neat trick with the dead ball. The longest measured homer is Mantle's 565-foot right-handed blast off Chuck Stobbs in Washington's Griffith Stadium in 1955. Unmeasured home runs have a way of getting longer. Babe Ruth allegedly hit a 600-foot homer in

Tampa; to read accounts of it, you might think it was still going.

Sockalexis faced Rusie at the Polo Grounds, an earlier version of the same stadium where Willie Mays played. Some accounts say Rusie boasted of his intention to strike out the "Redskin," and that the papers were full of fight talk, as if this were Buffalo Bill's "first scalp for Custer," Cody's killing of Yellow Hand after the Little Bighorn, which made the scout's reputation and enhanced his show-business career.

The newspapers of the day give the impression that fans liked Sockalexis. He never seems to have responded to "ki-yi's" and war whoops, and fans may have liked that. Perhaps, as with all stereotypes, when people actually saw a flesh-and-blood Indian who wasn't in a circus, their attitudes changed. Maybe, as later with Jackie Robinson, they respected the ballplayer, and learned to judge the man as a man. The papers, of course, may have whitewashed the way Sockalexis was treated.

Sockalexis hit third and faced Rusie in the top of the first. This was the Indian's first at-bat in New York, and seems to be the one verifiable event in Sockalexis's career. I suspected that he had hit a home run off Rusie, but that the length and majesty of the homer had been obscured by time. A 600-foot home run in 1897 was highly unlikely.

One newspaper account didn't mention the home run except in the box score, which at least proves Sockalexis hit one. *The New York Times,* however, ran a subhead, "Sockalexis' Usual Home

Run," which is revealing about the man's impact and reputation, considering he hit only three big-league home runs. "It is quite evident," the paper of record said, "that Sockalexis, the Indian, whose phenomenal stick work has been one of the surprises of the season, has been giving the other Cleveland players some of his ideas on how base hits should be made." The home run was described as "a beautiful drive over the right field ropes." A dramatic home run, yes; a mythical blast, no.

Ethnic teams are fun to argue about, but it can be difficult to tell what group a person actually came from. Two all-time great players with Irish surnames are actually Orangemen. Name these two Protestant greats, who are both associated with the city of Boston.

On July 3, Sockalexis was hitting .335, and then disaster struck. After having not missed two games in a row all season, Sockalexis missed two, played, missed another, played two more, missed two weeks, came back for games on July 24 and 25, and then played in only three more games that year. His major-league career, for all practical purposes, was over.

The reason was drink. One common misconception about Sockalexis that has been retold often enough to warrant refuting is that he hadn't tasted liquor until the day he made a great catch in Cleveland and grateful Spider fans took him to a tavern. Then, so this story goes, being an Indian, Sockalexis was as doomed as Hamlet. This tale absolves all who were involved in his decline, even Sockalexis himself, and puts the blame on chemistry.

In 1982, I visited Indian Island in Old Town, Maine, and saw Sockalexis's grave, in a small country cemetery. I asked about him at the Historical Society. An eighty-eight-year-old woman named Miss Violet (whether that was her first or last name I don't know) said she remembered "Louie" from her girlhood. Miss Violet corroborated what others have said about his being a gentle person, but pointed out that she never saw him drunk or after sundown. Miss Violet also said he had a reputation as a drinker at Holy Cross, and the Crusaders' coach used to post players at the corners of Sockalexis's bed to keep him from searching the night for liquor. She told me Sockalexis was reputed to have thrown a ball from Oak Hill on Indian Island that hit the smokestack of the Jordan Lumber Mill. Miss Violet thought "Louie" might have ranked with Babe Ruth if he hadn't been a drinker, but doubted he threw a ball from Oak Hill to the lumber company, because it is a distance of 4,000 feet.

Sockalexis's reputation as a drinker before he reached Cleveland is significant because it puts in focus the pressures he felt, being an Indian in the big league. If he was no stranger to liquor, why the rapid deterioration after July 4, 1897? He probably got hurt. It's difficult to learn about injuries from 1890s papers because of the use of euphemisms. If a man had "malaria," chances were good he actually had venereal disease. "Pneumonia" frequently stood for what in Boston is still referred to as "Irish pneumonia," which means complications arising from alcoholism. Sockalexis probably did get hurt, and then the question is why didn't he recover? Drink is undoubtedly part of the answer. Something happened over the Fourth of July. Sockalexis may have gone on a spree and hurt himself. What effect the war whoops, foot-stomping, "ki-yi's," and feathers had on him one can only surmise. We know he drank in college, and maybe he drank more when he saw the bright lights of the big league. He may have played drunk, and he may have played drunk and hurt. Sockalexis was either driven by demons, divinely indifferent to his talent, or sickened at some level he may not have understood by being so good at the white man's favorite game.

Another misconception is that the Indian was hitting .400 and then succumbed to drink. This, like the single-drink theory, is also not true. Cappy Gagnon of the Society for American Baseball Research has researched Sockalexis as carefully as anyone alive. One of Gagnon's areas of expertise is major-league players who attended Notre Dame University, even those who attended for only a month. Gagnon is a figure in SABR not unlike Doc Powers—enthusiastic, magnetic, and a terrific researcher. Cappy followed Sockalexis through the 1897 season. He recorded each day's performance from each box score, as they appeared in *Sporting Life,* and discovered that the origin of the .400-to-.338 fall, the riches-to-rags archetype that dominates all discussion of Sockalexis, is the *Sporting Life* August 7, 1897, list of "League Batsmen." That list has some impressive names. Wagner of Louisville, called Hans then and not yet trusted to play short, is the leader at .475. Ed Delahanty was hitting .424. Delahanty is paired with Sockalexis in "The Wild Irishman and the Gentle Indian," a chapter of Robert Smith's 1947 book *Baseball,* which was included in the first *Fireside Book of Baseball* (my own and many others' first exposure to literate baseball history). Both ballplayers came to bad ends: Delahanty, who, after a great thirteen-year career, met violent and/or accidental death with a plunge off a railroad trestle into Niagara Falls, and Sockalexis, the gentle, drunken might-have-been. On August 7, 1897, Delahanty had 151 hits in 356 at-bats, which computes to .424. Sockalexis was next, listed at .413. Cappy noticed that the Indian's average was computed by dividing 151 hits into 365 at-bats. He also noticed that not only was Sockalexis's hit total identical with Delahanty's, but also his runs, doubles, triples, and home runs. Gagnon decided this was too much of a coincidence, so he reconstructed the Indian's season from box scores, and discovered that Sockalexis was actually hitting .335 on August 7, which is consistent with the .338 the *Encyclopedia* lists for his final average.

Whatever happened to Sockalexis over the Fourth of July was so severe that he simply couldn't play anymore. His season wasn't a matter of hitting .400, beginning to drink, slipping, and then being benched. He steadily hit between .330 and .350, and then was benched. Whatever happened over the Fourth, in hotel rooms or saloons, was irreversible. Gagnon speculates that the team may have locked Sockalexis in a hotel room (shades of Holy Cross!) to keep him from drink, and the Indian may have injured himself jumping off a roof. The source of this theory is a report in an August *Sporting Life* that Sockalexis was recovering from a foot injury.

The 1890s have a reputation, doubtless enhanced by John McGraw's many years of talking to New York newspapermen, as the roughest, drunkest, brawlingest decade in the game's history. There's no question that the game was rough—ballplayers have always been a hard-drinking, and now a hard-drugging, lot—but judging from Sockalexis's disappearance from the Spiders lineup, when drink affected a man's performance, he didn't play. In one of Sockalexis's last games in 1897, on July 12, *Sporting Life* reported that his "miserable work in right field was responsible for Boston's six runs."

In August, the same publication wrote, "Much of the stuff written about his dalliance with grape juice and trysts with pale-faced maidens is purely speculation." By August, Sockalexis was a disaster. It didn't take long for the press to gloat. After all, he was now living out the stereotype of the drunken Indian. No longer was Louis Sockalexis a natural man and country boy, no longer was he some Huckleberry Finn "noble savage" with a touch of Horatio Alger; he turned into Huck's gutter-drunk Pap before their very eyes, and it only proved what they'd know all along about Indians. A Providence paper summed it all up with a pun: "Curved balls are not the sort of benders that have kept the Redman down."

Eighteen ninety-seven was the end of the American holocaust. So many Indians had been killed, it wasn't necessary to kill any more. There had once been four million Indians; now there were 800,000. Oppressors revel in the vices of the oppressed. The drunken Indian excused the broken treaties, stolen land, and shattered cultures. Sockalexis's career began in stereotype with war whoops and "ki-yi's," reached its apex in June against Rusie ("Sockalexis' Usual Home Run"), and descended into stereotype by August. He drank himself out of the big league. After partial seasons at Waterbury-Bristol, Hartford, and Lowell, he drank himself out of the minor leagues. His minor-league career lasted four years. His big-league career lasted 94 games.

Henry Adams said the historian's business was to "follow the track of the energy," and the track of so much energy runs through the brief story of Louis Sockalexis that it's difficult to read just what kind of story it was. It's not a nice story. Louis Sockalexis was a representative of a slaughtered race who played the masters' favorite game better than the masters—but he was no Jackie Robinson. He played in no melting pot. He was no bridge, no messenger, no redeemer. He appeared at a time when baseball was replacing the frontier in the American psyche, when a population no longer able to go west was learning to live within boundaries—physical, psychological, even spiritual—and he could have been great. Sockalexis excited the kranks in a way no other rookie ever had, but he disappeared into the Indian burial ground of the bottle, and remains, even now, a riddle.

Answers to questions in the preceding chapter:

- Oscar Bielaski played four years with the National Association, from 1871 to 1875, and in the first year of the National League, 1876.

- Eddie Abbaticchio appeared in 1897. This is also the year Sockalexis started, and perhaps the Indian drew some attention from the Italian.

- Babe Ruth, Honus Wagner, Lou Gehrig, and Mike Schmidt were all Germans.

- Eddie Collins, longtime Red Sox general manager, and Mickey Cochrane, who attended Boston University, were both Irish Protestants.

Brothers and Fathers

ONE type of question that has no relevance to winning, losing, or changing styles of play involves sets of brothers. Part of the interest in "brothers" questions is that most of us grew up playing baseball with siblings. Roger Angell says being a baseball fan is like being part of an enormous family. The players are the younger members—they have adventures and make news, while the retired players and fans make up a huge extended family. It's fun to ask questions about actual families in this large metaphorical family.

The rarity of brothers good enough to play in the big leagues also makes these questions interesting. Nick Carraway's father said fundamental human decency is parceled out unequally at birth, and the same is true for athletic ability. It's amazing when the lightning of baseball ability strikes once in a family, let alone two or three times.

Who were the first brothers elected to the Hall of Fame?

The answer is not the Waners, who were inducted in 1952 and '67, but those baseball pioneers Harry and George Wright, who were enshrined in 1937 (Harry was elected in the Hall's second year) and 1953.

George and Harry Wright were pioneers of the professional game. Their father was a cricket player who came to America to coach the English game. The sons abandoned the father's game to perfect the native one. Harry, the older, played outfield and managed, while George was a shortstop. They were the backbone of the famed Cincinnati Reds (1869–70), the first and most successful openly professional team, and then of the Boston National Association Red Stockings (1871–75), who dominated the first openly professional league.

Asking which brothers hit the most home runs is too easy. Even a fan who doesn't remember Tommy Aaron, Henry's slick-fielding, light-hitting first-baseman brother, would be wise to guess the Aarons, because if Hank had a brother who hit just one, they would head the list. Tommy hit only 13, but that gives the Aarons 768, which puts them 95 in front of the next brothers. Asking for the brothers with the second-most home runs is also too easy. Any moderately informed fan should guess the DiMaggios because there were three of them, and Joe hit 361 homers. What's not so well known is that the eldest DiMaggio, Vince, who had the least talent ("Joe is the best hitter, Dom is the best fielder, and Vince has the best singing voice"), hit 125 home runs. Dom, who has the distinction of stealing the fewest bases to lead a league (15 in 1950), had a .298 life BA, and hit 87.

Two pairs of brothers are tied for third most career home runs with 444. Who are they?

This is a better question and requires a review of memory data. It is fun to figure out because, whoever they are, these brothers are not going to be obscure. Home-run feats are all post-1920, and home runs are not subtle. They are celebrated, especially in large numbers. The most difficult homer questions ask for least, not most. Who had the fewest home runs to lead a league since 1920? If you guess that this happened during the Second World War, when 4-Fs, graybeards, and boys, as they said, stocked the major leagues, you're right. Nick Etten led the American League with 22 in 1944. Wee Tommy Leach of the 1902 Pirates had the fewest to lead in the twentieth century, with six.

   Which set of brothers ranks third? One way to attack this question is to think of brother combinations, fraternal trinities. The DiMaggios are not the only big-league trio. There were the Alous—two banjo hitters and Felipe, who hit 206 homers and was one of the very good players in the NL in an age of giants. Felipe and Matty are two of only five National Leaguers to hit .300 in 1968, the year of the pitcher. (Naming those five is a good question because it celebrates an unheralded feat. The NL batting champ—and one must give him his due, because the AL champ hit .301—was Pete Rose, at .335. The others were the two Alous at .332 and .317; Alex Johnson, who later beat Carl Yastrzemski out of a fourth BA title on the last day of the 1970 season; and Curt Flood, baseball's forgotten rebel, who hit .301.)

Hitting .300 in 1968 was no small accomplishment. Only one man in the entire American League, Carl Yastrzemski, did it. This saved the AL the disgrace of being the only big league ever led with an average under .300. Prior to 1968, the lowest champion average was Elmer Flick's .306 for Cleveland in '06.

Two Alou brothers hit .300 in '68, and Jesus, whose name made us all laugh before we realized that it was one of the most common in the hemisphere, hit .292. Pete Rose and Felipe Alou were the only big-leaguers who got 200 hits that year. The Alou brothers, who will always be remembered for having played each outfield position simultaneously in a game in 1963, hit 265 homers, which puts them ninth.

What family had the most brothers in the major leagues, and how many home runs did they hit?

No less than five Delahantys played in the big leagues: Ed, Joe, Frank, Jim, and Tom. Big Ed was one of the best players of the nineteenth century. He had a .346 life BA and hit 100 dead-ball home runs. Unfortunately, his brothers managed to hit only 27 homers among them, which places them

166

twentieth on the brothers list, and first on the dead-ball brothers list.

The third best set is not the Waners. Paul and Lloyd are the best average-hitting brothers. They hit .325 between them, but in spite of being called "Big Poison" and "Little Poison," Paul weighed 148 pounds, and his brother was smaller. They hit only 140 homers.

The third most homering brothers are Ken and Clete Boyer, and Lee and Carlos May. Ken Boyer almost has Hall of Fame stats. He played a very good third base (one of the most underrepresented positions in the Hall), and hit 282 homers. Clete, who was a superb third baseman, hit 162. This is a nice piece of information because good players can be forgotten, and who would have thought Clete Boyer hit 162 home runs? Anyone who saw the younger Boyer remembers his sensational fielding. If there were a Fielding Hall of Fame, or if the Hall had a fielding wing, Clete would be in it. He was the only third baseman of his time comparable to Brooks Robinson, but his hitting seemed comparable to Milt Bolling or Fay Throneberry. Good questions force us to dig, and digging reveals that Clete Boyer hit 162 home runs.

Lee and Carlos May hit 444 homers. This answer commemorates a solid slugger, Lee May, who hit 354 HRs, and his younger brother Carlos, who is a might-have-been. Carlos hit 18 homers in 100 games of his rookie year, 1969, and looked as if he was as good as his brother, but the top of Carlos's thumb was blown off in a mortar accident that summer. Young men had to do something about military service in 1969, and Carlos May was in the reserves. He returned the next season. There were skin-graft operations in which part of Carlos May's stomach was grafted onto his thumb. A teammate said the sight of it made him sick. Carlos wore a special batting glove that extended his lost thumb to provide a better grip while batting. He played for ten years, hitting .308 in '72, but never with the power he showed in his rookie year.

What catcher, who is in the Hall of Fame, hit fewer home runs than his brother, who was a pitcher?

Rick Ferrell, a 1985 inductee, and .281 lifetime hitting catcher, played from 1929 until 1947 (that average is the equivalent of hitting .261 now), and hit 28 career home runs. His brother Wes, who won 193 games and had a .601 lifetime winning percentage, hit 38 home runs, which is the career record for pitchers. Wes Ferrell also holds the season record for homers by a pitcher with nine, which he did for the Red Sox in 1931.

The Old Timers' Committee of the Hall selected Rick Ferrell. There are two kinds of players in Cooperstown: those who people thought were Hall of Famers while they played, and who were voted in by writers who saw them play within fifteen years of their retirement; and players no one thought were Hall of Fame caliber, who get in through the Old Timers' Committee. This is a shame because the Hall of Fame is important. Cooperstown is baseball's past made visible, and the shrine shouldn't cheapen itself.

When Rick Ferrell was inducted, his fielding was cited. Men certainly should be able to field their way into the Hall, but only if they're the standard by which others are judged, like Ozzie Smith. I've never heard a catcher compared to Rick Ferrell. His ability to handle the knuckleball was mentioned. If that's a criterion, how about Bob Uecker? He caught Wilhelm as well as anyone in Hoyt's long, long career.

In 1987, Cal and Billy Ripken became only the third set of brothers to play shortstop and second base for the same team at the same time. Who are the others?

Most of us have played beside our brothers and can identify with siblings facing the opposition together. Brothers are not rare in baseball. There have been pitching brothers and battery brothers (did you know that Bobby Shantz and Larry Sherry had brothers who caught them?), but for brothers to form a double-play combination is rare. One set were twins, which is a clue for card collectors.

Eddie and Johnny O'Brien were identical twins who starred in basketball at Seattle University and then signed with the Pirates. Johnny lasted six years in the major leagues and Eddie five, mostly as fringe players, but the idea of twins playing short and second for the same team inspired Topps to issue its first multiple-player card.

The other brothers were Granny and Wes

Hamner of the '45 Phillies. Granny went on to a 17-year career, while Wes lasted only 32 games.

How many sets of twins have played major-league baseball?

This is hardly an ultimate question, but the answer is four. George and Bill Hunter, a pitcher and an outfielder, had brief careers around 1910. Claude and Clarence Jonnard, a pitcher and a catcher, had short careers in the twenties; Ray and Roy Grimes played in the twenties; and the O'Briens played in the fifties. Ray Grimes is the only twin who was a star. He hit .329 over six seasons, but his career was cut short by injury. Ray holds the record for driving in runs in 22 consecutive games. Roy played in only 26 games. No one has determined whether any of these twins (other than the O'Briens) were identical.

Jose Canseco has an identical twin, Ozzie, who is a minor-league outfielder in the A's system. It's interesting that men with identical genetic makeup can have had such different careers.

Donald Hall, in a wonderfully titled essay, "Fathers Playing Catch with Sons," says football is brothers beating up on each other and baseball is fathers playing catch with sons. Baseball is certainly a mythical estate passed through the generations, but baseball is learned as much from brothers as from fathers. Fathers don't pass on everything they know. There's a gulf between a man and his father that doesn't exist between a man and his brother. James Agee ends the prologue to *A Death in the*

Family, a novel about a father's death, with an account of an eight-year-old's feelings about his family: "After a little I am taken in and put to bed. Sleep . . . draws me unto her: and those receive me, who quietly treat me, as one familiar and well-beloved in that home: but will not, oh, will not, not now, not ever; but will not ever tell me who I am."

Just as fathers can't or won't tell you who you are, so they don't tell everything about baseball. Baseball you learn for yourself, and from your brothers. Sartre said that the most disillusioned statement he ever heard was "Charity begins at home." Think about that for a minute. There is a built-in inequality between father and son. One perceives himself as either superior or inferior to his father. It's not a matter of equals.

What father-and-son combination had the most hits?

This is interesting because it leads to the most equal father and son. The strategy that helped answer the question of which set of brothers hit the most home runs is no help. No man with over 3,500 hits has had a son play, and fathers with multiple big-league sons are not the answer. The Sislers amassed 3,557 hits, and would have been the leader, but George, one of the greatest of all hitters, suffered an eye injury and finished with "only" 2,812 hits, and one of his sons, Dave, was a pitcher. Dixie and Harry Walker are sons of a major-leaguer, Ewart Walker, but Ewart was a pitcher, so that family ranks only fifth with 2,883. Logic dictates that the famous fathers and not-so-famous sons, like Yogi and Dale Berra, Maury and Bump Wills, or Eddie Collins senior and junior, will not be the answer because the famous father would not have been able to get enough hits to compensate for a negligible son. Even Eddie Collins's 3,311 hits cannot salvage his son's 66.

Are there any fathers and sons who each had long careers? Another way to approach the question is to think of a son who was the equal of, or better than, his father. This leads to Gus and Buddy Bell. Gus played fifteen years, and Buddy played his eighteenth season in 1988. They had 4,344 hits after '88, and 407 home runs, which ties them with the Berras. Buddy had the misfortune to play on terrible Indian and Ranger teams, and in Texas Stadium before the walls that cut the prevailing wind were put up. The younger Bell was always an excellent third baseman, and had he played in better places, he might be a candidate for the Hall of Fame.

On paper, the Bells' careers look remarkably equal, but Gus, who hit .281, played in a bandbox at Crosley Field in a lineup of sluggers, while Buddy, whose life BA is .281, had to carry weak teams in big stadiums.

What father and son won the most games? Have a father and son ever won a hundred games apiece in the big leagues?

These questions reveal an interesting piece of information. Fathers and sons have been more equal in pitching than in hitting. Four pairs won around 200 games, and only one, the Walshes, is carried by the more famous member (Ed senior won 195, Ed junior only 11). The other pairs are more equal, but no one is a Hall of Famer. Dizzy and Steve Trout had 254 wins after '88, and Steve was still active. Jim Bagby *père* and *fils,* the forgotten 30-game winner and the son who helped stop Joe DiMaggio's hitting streak, won 224 between them, with the father winning 127 and the son 97. The last pair to approach 200 wins, with 194, features a son who won more games than his father: Joe Coleman, Jr., with 142 and Joe senior with 52.

I prefer "brother" questions because the rivalry is usually more evenly matched. This isn't to say that sibling rivalry isn't fierce, or that a brother's love isn't ambivalent, but the dark side of fatherhood is darker. Huck Finn isn't terrorized by his brother. There is one great father-and-son fact: Herman Pillette and his son Duane led the American League in losses twenty-eight years apart.

With the Perrys and now the Niekros, we no longer have Henry Mathewson to kick around. The answer to the question "Which pair of brothers won the most games in this century?" used to be Christy and Henry Mathewson. Christy won 373, and Henry, who pitched only three games, won none. In one of those games, Henry did succeed in walking 14 batters, which is still a record. There is something both amusing and satisfying in Henry Mathewson, because we all learned the game in forgotten backyards with brothers and friends and their brothers, and all know the competitiveness and complex devotion that go into loving a brother. At the same time one absolutely adores him, it's hard not to think he's a jerk.

Christy Mathewson 373
Henry Mathewson 0

In our dreams we aren't Tommy Aaron or Ron Allen or John Faulkner when we can be Hank Aaron, Dick Allen, or William Faulkner. Have you ever heard Chris Jagger sing? Major-league brothers are usually so polarized—as with Graig and Jim Nettles—that it's a pleasure to find evenly matched brothers.

Who are the six pairs of brothers with combined life averages over .300?

The Waners lead the list at .325. They played in the twenties and thirties and stayed around for the lean war years, so the absolute value of their average would have to be scaled down, but for old-fashioned, missionary position, unweighted statistics, the Waners lead the next brothers by 14 points.

Two of these family combinations are amazingly well matched. Long Bob Meusel played 11 seasons and hit .309; his brother Irish played 11 seasons and hit .310. The Meusels, who were such notables in New York baseball in the twenties, are now mostly forgotten, except that one played in the same outfield as Babe Ruth, and had a better arm; and the other played under a great manager alongside a great manager-to-be, having been managed by John McGraw while sharing the outfield with Casey Stengel.

There's something nice about equal brothers. It's the good side of sibling rivalry—the camaraderie and us-against-the-world side that appears so rarely in the major leagues. What pair of brothers, who each played over ten years, hit an identical lifetime .296? They weren't equal hitters. The younger hit 288 homers while the older hit 58. The younger also had the colorful nickname "Indian." Like the Waners, these brothers were from the hard-packed dirt playing fields of Oklahoma, where most everyone has Native American ancestors. The equal-average brothers were Bob and Roy Johnson.

What pair of brothers, who hit .303 together, each won a batting title? Though the answer does not reveal a statistical trend or change in the way the game was played, there is a nice blend of obscure answer and unobscure category. These brothers led the National League within four years of each other. The older has the distinction of making a dumb remark about the integration of baseball, and the younger of turning a man coming off successive seasons of .231, .264, and .145 into a batting champ 19 years after he won it himself.

The champion brothers are Ewart's sons, Dixie and Harry Walker. Dixie won a war-year title ('44), but may be best remembered for the irony in his answer to a question about the desegregation of baseball when he said he wouldn't mind a Negro in the league "as long as he isn't with the Dodgers." Harry Walker, whose acerbic tongue and ability to teach a certain style of banjo hitting got Matty Alou the crown in '66, won the title in 1947, which makes him the only man in NL history to win the title and be traded in the same season. Harry also hit the single in the '46 Series that Dom DiMaggio's heavy-legged replacement, Leon Culberson, relayed to Johnny Pesky, who held it—contemplating, no doubt, the curse the Boston Red Sox have labored under since selling Babe Ruth—thereby allowing Enos Slaughter to score the Series-winning run in a cloud of dust.

The other .300-hitting brothers are the Delahantys at .311 (Ed is the only one over .300, but he hit .346), the O'Rourkes, who hit .309 together but played mostly in the nineteenth century, and the Aarons, who hit .300 because Hank's fine career compensated for Tommy's .229.

No discussion of brothers would be complete without Jay Hanna Dean and Paul Dee Dean, who, as Dizzy and Daffy, were a kind of hard-throwing, cracker Marx Brothers during the worst years of the Depression. The Deans may not be the brothers with the best nicknames—George and Lewis Wiltse were known as "Hooks" and "Snake"—but the Deans are the most famous brothers. (What's more fun than looking up names in the *Encyclopedia?* It out-begats the Bible.) Curt Gowdy called Dizzy "baseball's greatest showman after Babe Ruth." Dizzy Dean lived out one of the less complicated American archetypes, the crafty country illiterate who wows 'em in the city. The older Dean is also a baseball archetype: all-time great for two or three seasons. Like Joe Wood and Sandy Koufax, Dizzy Dean was phenomenal for a brief time. Wood had one great year. (He was 34–5 and won 3 World Series games in 1912.) Koufax had three complete great seasons; Dizzy Dean had two, but Dizzy had the right personality, played on the right team, and had a brother. Part of Dizzy's down-home charm may be that he was everyone's wild older brother. Dizzy and Daffy had only two good years together. In 1934 and 1935 Dizzy won 30 and 28 while Paul won 19 each year. The 49 games they won in '34 is most by brothers in the same season. Like the Waners, the Deans are the good side of sibling rivalry, the us-against-the-world side that so few brothers achieve.

Cardboard Madeleines

NEITHER standard history of baseball has much to say about baseball cards. This is an inexplicable oversight because the track of the game's energy runs squarely through these cardboard icons. We all collected them—some of us still do—and many of us lament that our collections, once so eagerly gathered, so carefully sorted, banded, traded, and flipped, have, like our childhoods, disappeared. By the 1980s, adults were spending more money on cards than children were. The question, which my wife asks of my own collecting, and which this chapter will try to answer, is why.

What was the first baseball card?

This is a difficult question. Cards, like the game itself, did not start in one place. They evolved from "trade cards," which were a nineteenth-century form of advertising that had a lithograph on one side and an advertisement on the other, and were distributed by salesmen or left on shop counters. These cards depicted everything from products to places, stores, or factories. Some had writing, others only pictures, and some had blank spaces where advertising could be stamped on. They were the calling cards of a highly mercantile pre-electronic culture. Many of the early depictions of baseball were humorous, and made fun of men playing a child's game. Babies were shown hit by baseballs or arguing with umpires. "Trade cards" were very popular after the Civil War and, by 1880, were the most collected objects in America. The baseball card was once only one of many collected cards.

Looking for the first baseball card is like looking for the oldest human remains. Discoveries keep pushing back our ancestors. For years it was thought an 1869 card showing ten members of the Cincinnati Reds was the oldest card. This neatly tied in with the notion of professional baseball starting in the Queen City, and, given all the records Pete Rose bagged, made Cincinnati a sort of alpha and omega of baseball, but a card has been found featuring nine Brooklyn Atlantics, dated 1868, so the Wright brothers and their Cincinnati team have been supplanted by a card featuring such Brooklyn notables as Dicky Pearce, who is credited with inventing the bunt, and Joe Start, the first great first baseman. Nineteenth-century researcher Mark Rucker has discovered a card of the first nationally known player, James Creighton, issued by the Peck & Snyder Sporting Goods Co. in 1863. Whether this card was available to the public in a way that would qualify it as a baseball card in any sense we would recognize is debatable. Creighton, who played for the Brooklyn Excelsiors, is credited with adding a wrist snap to his pitches, which revolutionized pitching, and reputedly once went a whole season without being put out. As if these feats weren't legendary enough, like some doomed mythological hero, Creighton died from internal injuries suffered hitting a home run. Whether Creighton or the Atlantics are featured on the first card, it's fitting that the first card should come from the Northeast, since the game began there.

It's interesting that "trade cards" were collected by nineteenth-century adults, but this still doesn't explain why twentieth-century males collect baseball cards. The economic factor, though minor, can't be discounted. Cards may be a poor man's Wall Street, but speculating in a commodity, however humble, adds spice to the hobby. The urge to possess starts early. Children don't collect merely to identify with their heroes. They hoard, trade, sell, buy, and enjoy the thrill of possession. One could argue that along with the game of Monopoly, baseball cards prepare the American male for capitalism as successfully as the public schools.

What is the most expensive card?

This question demonstrates the extent to which collecting is not child's play. The most valuable card is the 1909 Honus Wagner, from the American Tobacco Company issue of 1909–11, known to collectors as T-206. The card is called T-206 after the system devised by Jefferson Burdick in *The American Card Catalog*. Burdick compiled a listing not only for baseball cards, but for all cards. His book was the result of a lifelong obsession. Burdick gave his card collection to the Metropolitan Museum of Art, and it fills 660 albums. The great collector worked in a factory in Syracuse, New York. He was an encyclopedist, one of those driven men, like Dr. Johnson or Darwin or Ernie Lanigan, the man Damon Runyon called Figger Filbert, who compiled the first baseball encyclopedia in the 1920s. It's odd how men like Lanigan, who did such basic things as codify our numerical memory, or Curt Flood, who started the twentieth-century players' revolt, just aren't remembered.

Why Burdick called the American Tobacco Company cards T-206 is unclear. The *T* presumably stands for "tobacco." The figure 206 does not refer to the number of cards in the set, which is 522. It's nice that there is something mysterious about the most expensive card, besides the outrageous sum it commands. The card is rare because it was withdrawn from circulation at Wagner's request. He didn't smoke cigarettes and didn't want to set a bad example for the country's youth. He also wasn't paid. In 1988, that card, in mint condition, sold at auction for $110,000.

Why do adults collect baseball cards?

I started again at the age of thirty-six. Between thirteen and thirty-five I was a lapsed collector. I wanted to collect, but suppressed the urge. I would buy a package or two every year to see what they looked like—and each year they looked worse, and seemed further and further away from the artwork, feel, and colors of the magical cards of the mid-

184

fifties. Then, in 1983, I decided I didn't care how it looked or what people thought, and bought the whole Topps set. I did it half as a joke, or told myself it was a joke—who but a philistine would buy the whole set, instead of putting it together one piece at a time, like an artist? This was like opening presents before Christmas or cheating in school, but after the 792 cards were organized by team and put in plastic sheets in two notebooks, I was hooked. There was satisfaction in having the whole set, in having completed the circle. It was all there, organized, indestructible, and retrievable. I felt like the master of time and space.

The next step was organizing the old cards in a battered suitcase that I'd carried with me for thirty years. I went back to the pawnshop in downtown Boston where I'd bought the notebooks and plastic sheets. This was a concession to macho—no hobby store for me, but a place where high school kids pawn class rings and guys who need a shave hock anything that glistens. Those cards survived countless moves, climate changes, and the ravages of time in that suitcase, which, like the portrait of Dorian Gray, became decrepit while the cards remained the same. As I surveyed these relics, now viewable and as safe from the modern world as any of us, I realized they meant more to me now than they did then. As my wife says, "Why?"

Why children collect is easier to understand. Baseball cards are "neat," as we used to say. They were the big leagues in miniature, and you owned part of them. If you had Ted Williams, you had Ted Williams. There wasn't another part of the adult

185

world that could be had like that. I tried stamps but lost interest. Coins seemed grown up because they had obvious value, but they lacked personality. Baseball cards were like owning stock in the season. Your favorites did well or they didn't. Wally Post could go from the top of the Cincinnati stack to the front spokes of your bicycle. Cards were hostages to fortune. You picked players you liked, and their strengths, at some important moment in the vague, heroic future, might be yours.

They also had information. We used to study the backs. I remember arguing that the '57s were superior to the '56s because they had year-by-year stats on the back, not just the most recent season and lifetime totals.

Before trying to answer definitively why adults collect, let's ask more questions.

What is the first Topps card set?

When most of us think of baseball cards, we think of Topps, the Brooklyn chewing-gum company that has dominated the market since the fifties. Topps didn't make cards until 1951, and that first set, the "blue-backs" and "red-backs," were designed to look like a card game. They weren't strictly baseball cards. The next year Topps was less squeamish about competing directly with Bowman, the Philadelphia company that had been issuing baseball cards, and produced the '52 set, the most valuable Topps set. The '52s list at over $36,000, and contain the most expensive post–World War II card, the famous Topps number 311, the '52 Mantle, which is worth over $6,500. Mantle went back to the minors in '52 and production of the card stopped, making it rare.

What is the best affordable set?

My favorite set is the '56. They are the last cards in which artists hand-tinted black-and-white photos to produce the illusion of a color photograph. This set contains the penultimate collection of New York Giants and Brooklyn Dodgers. The action shots are in the old ballparks. Some of the outfield walls, like the one Roberto Clemente is leaping against, have advertising. This is a set for connoisseurs.

This is also the last year of good reverse-side cartoons. A triptych summarized the highlights of each player's career or life, which meant someone went to the trouble to do a narrative and story-board. The cartoons contain humor and wit. A young Clemente is given the Brooklyn Bridge by a man with a contract in his hand, and the caption reads, "Roberto was first signed by the Dodgers for a bonus." A scout holding a contract behind his back watches a young batter through a knothole on the back of Harmon Killebrew's card. Killebrew had only 93 career at-bats at the time, but the card informs us, "The Senators feel Harmon will be a big star," and a big-bellied, black-hatted U.S. senator is shown with a hand on each of Harmon's shoulders. My childhood favorite was a sinking ship on Cubs outfielder Frank Kellert's card: "Frank had a close call when a troopship he was on was torpedoed in World War II." Those cartoons were full of men wearing crowns to show they had led a league in some category; there were balls hopping over bats, pitches making circles in the air, balls hit so hard they sprouted wings, balls flying out of stadiums and over cities, wearing a mortarboard and tassel to show that a player had been to college, or bandaged because they'd been hit so hard. The artists caught some zany childhood sense of visualized jargon.

The '56s were horizontal rather than vertical, as all subsequent regular-issue sets have been. The horizontal format was inspired by Topps's competitor, Bowman. A card war raged between the two companies between '52 and '55, and Topps responded by making its cards horizontal. Topps also made its cards bigger, like Chevrolet having bigger fins than Ford. The first year Topps had no competition was 1956. The Brooklyn company bought out the Philadelphia company after four years of lawsuits; and Topps, like the National League in the 1890s, ruled alone until 1980, when a lawsuit opened the market by denying Topps a monopoly on cards sold with bubble gum. The 1980s, like the 1880s, have three major leagues: Topps, Donruss, and Fleer. Like the National League in the 1880s, Topps holds the preeminent position.

What's the most common complaint of collectors?

There's a dark side to collecting. Almost every American male collected, sorted, organized, and possessed these now-valuable relics (it was amazing how compulsive even slobs could be), and entrusted them, sorted and banded, to a closet. As we grew up

—the big suburban generation, sons of World War II vets who did well as the American economy expanded—and left home, those closets filled with '54 Aarons, '55 Clementes, and '56 Mantles (even '52 Mantles!) were cleaned out by our long-suffering mothers, who, following the admonition of the Apostle Paul, thought we had reached an age to put away childish things but, in fact, to paraphrase Our Lord, they knew not what they did. Out went the shoe boxes with their carefully sorted, banded cargo —out with jars of marbles and bales of comic books, out with all the flora, fauna, pennants, totems, and paraphernalia of childhood that we once couldn't live without and thought we'd save forever. Now, like the past itself, the shoe boxes and cards are gone; unlike the past, the cards and comic books are worth money. This is the Oedipal tragedy of the 1980s.

There's a catch, of course. For all the middle-aged men I've heard at stores and shows lamenting the untimely loss of their collections (mothers are inevitably blamed for what came out of the closet), there is a definite catch. If it's value—cold, hard lucre—that a man is mourning, not souvenirs of his past, if it's cash rather than lost time we lament, mother-scorners are probably grieving for no good reason, because dealers and collectors want pristine cards. Value is determined by condition. The most expensive cards are the hobby's equivalent of the little old lady's car that was only driven to church. Only perfect cards—perfect corners, perfectly centered, with no scratches, and some collectors look for these things with magnifying glasses—bring top

189

dollar. Cards held by rubber bands become "notched," as collectors say, or at least the top and bottom card in a stack do. God forbid a card has been handled and shows signs of wear like a saint's bones. Adults do not worship with their fingers; they admire untouched perfection behind plastic or glass.

No one pays good money for cards that look as if they belonged to real children. What self-respecting, bike-riding child of the 1950s kept his cards in pristine condition? Who didn't flip cards? Or play "leaners" or "face up, face down"? How many ways does a child have of testing the laws of gravity, and every one of them bent the corners and scratched the perfect surfaces of those now-valuable cards. The hobby papers talk about finds of unopened cards, boxes in attics that haven't seen the light of day or the clammy touch of an excited youngster since 1955, or uncut sheets overlooked by the manufacturer that will now be sliced like money fresh from the mint. Wherever these cards come from, it's not from anyone I knew.

The business of baseball cards is a business. It's run by adults. This isn't childhood. One doesn't get to return to fifth grade armed with an adult mind and *Beckett's Guide* to swindle your former schoolmates out of Mickey Mantle and Pete Rose cards. You're up against men who do this for a living, and they know just how much a man can want something. They know how defenseless a Roger Maris fetishist can be. They know how to squeeze a fellow who feels that the condition of his inner self rests on owning both Topps '54 Williamses. They know that some of us are just this side of Humbert Humbert in our inability to withstand an obsession. These potbellied men, who cast a jeweler's eye over their wares and have John D. Rockefeller's sense of pricing, control the very doors to the sanctuary. What did Philip Roth call baseball—"a secular church"? There are moneylenders in the temple.

When did these cardboard icons become truly valuable?

Baseball cards, like country music, made it in the 1980s. The hobby became a serious business, and there's money in it. A hundred 1980 Rickey Hendersons, which could be had for two cents apiece in '80, and for five dollars before he was traded to New York, are now worth $2,800. The idea of a money-making hobby appeals to people who will never make a lot of it unless they win a state lottery, which is most of us. In the early 1980s, card prices shot up. As a result of the Carter inflation of the late seventies, the price of all property, including real estate and collectibles, went up.

Which card is a player's most valuable card?

As card prices rose, the rookie card craze began. A star's first card—his first Topps card in particular —became his most valuable card. The craze was started by dealers. They needed cards that could be had by the thousands and that would appreciate in value quickly. A dealer was unlikely to be able to get a thousand Hank Aaron rookie cards (1954), but he could get a thousand Wade Boggses. Why the rookie card? Dealers needed one card for each player that would appreciate, and the rookie is an easy choice. A player's best year could have been his most valuable card, but that would mean collectors would have to be able to think, and the industry needed an unambiguous way to hike prices.

Collectors try to pick who will be the best rookie, and look in the weekly *Sports Collectors Digest* (the bible of collecting—a publication that has price lists updated every week), to buy in quantity. In December 1985, Jose Canseco cards (Donruss or Fleer; Topps knew he might be hot and held both Canseco and Walley Joyner out of the '86 regular issue to sweeten their "update" set, which is supposed to update traded players, but is actually a way to sucker collectors into spending another $12 for a 132-card set after they have spent $20 for 792 the previous winter) could be had in orders over a hundred for 20 cents apiece. By the end of the '86 season, these cards were selling for as much as $5. There is money to be made, if one gambles right and gambles quickly. Of course, there are men stuck with thousands of Mark Fidrych or Joe Charboneau cards.

What's the most expensive card of a player who played in the 1980s?

It has to be a rookie card, and the Pete Rose rookie in mint condition goes for $450. This, like the rookie fixation, is also a product of dealers and easily led consumers. There may be a million Rose

192

rookie cards, not all mint of course, but certainly enough so the price shouldn't be that high. The fact that the Rose card is so valuable says as much about those who collect as about those who sell: Pete Rose is exactly what we all apparently want. He's a hitter. Interestingly, pitchers never go as high as hitters. Steve Carlton's rookie card is $90. Pitching may be 70 percent of the game, but it's not 70 percent of the collecting game. Pitching may not be 70 percent of being a fan. Fantasizing about hitting may be the game's most basic form of hero worship.

The Rose rookie is a classic. It's a multiple-player card. Four hopeful faces framed by red circles look out from a yellow background. All four wistful young men might be stars, or, more likely none of them. Here's a good card question: who appears with Pete Rose on his inaugural card? If you guess that the other three are infielders, you're right. Remember that Pete broke in as a second baseman and was Rookie of the Year at that position. Two of his premier cardmates were second basemen. Pedro Gonzalez, one of the first players from San Pedro de Macorís, the city of 70,000 in the Dominican Republic that currently has 18 men in the big leagues, and who was traded to Cleveland where, for a while, he played next to Chico Salmon, who was the only major-leaguer I ever heard say he believed in ghosts. Al Weis was the other second sacker. Weis, who shared second with Ken Boswell on the "Miracle Mets" of '69, was a terrific fielder who couldn't hit. Weis hit only seven home runs in over 1,500 at-bats, but he hit one off Dave McNally in the World Series, which prompted a friend of mine to remark, "Anyone with a bat in his hands is dangerous." The other infielder was Ken McMullen, one of the men Washington got for Frank Howard. His career lasted 16 years.

Is the card market an accurate reflection of players' value?

Absolutely not. The rookie cards of players who attract attention to themselves command ridiculous sums. The Pete Rose rookie goes for $450, while Frank Robinson goes for $125. This tells us about the marketability of statistics. Frank Robinson was ten times the ballplayer Pete Rose was, but Frank didn't break a major record. Many collectors are middle-aged, and Pete appealed to middle-aged men because he was one. Rose slapped singles and huffed and puffed around the bases with his chest out, and every out-of-shape man in America said, "There but for the grace of God go I." No one ever accused dealers or collectors of imagination. Consider these rookie-card prices: Hank Aaron, '54 Topps, $650; Willie Mays, '51 Bowman, $1,250, '52 Topps, $875; Roberto Clemente, '55 Topps, $500. Tony Oliva's first card goes for $10, Rod Carew's for $125. The Luis Tiant rookie is $5, Tom Seaver $450. (Seaver was a better pitcher, but not ninety times better.) Joe Morgan is $30, Mike Schmidt $150. Dick Allen is $8, Steve Garvey $65. The list goes on. Several years ago a cache of counterfeit Rose rookie cards was uncovered in a suburb of Los Angeles (perfect place for it), and even these cards, duly marked as counterfeit, have hit the market. I bought one for $10, which was exactly what I thought a Rose rookie was worth.

Again, why do adults collect baseball cards?

Why do grown men collect? Why did grown men fall for the rookie-card ploy? The economic factor is part of it—economics always raises its ugly head, as Marx ably demonstrated—but we're not talking about oil wells; we're talking about two-and-a-half-by three-and-a-half-inch pieces of cardboard. Economics doesn't explain the tremendous urge that I, and other collectors, get to obtain cards. My wife thinks there ought to be someone I can call until the feeling passes. Why do I want cards in pristine condition? My original cards, the ones that have the highest sentimental value, are far from mint. What kind of accident is it that grown men want that version of a thing which looks like it's never been touched? It may have something to do with virginity, a rare commodity in America today.

Baseball cards may be tokens of the latency period, that pleasant age between ten and twelve when boys are "best friends" and girls are foreign objects. Are cards tickets back to the golden end of childhood, when the night force of sexuality was sublimated into friends and baseball? Perhaps the almost exclusively male world of trade publications, conventions, and card shows is an adult version of the "girl haters' club." Perhaps cards are subliminal reminders of a womanless, friend-filled, twelve-year-old world where sex was a wink, a joke, and a tall tale, not an obsession.

Adults do, however, collect more things than baseball cards. FDR was a stamp collector, and spent the afternoon of December 7, 1941, after receiving the news that the Japanese had bombed Pearl Harbor, working on his collection. The President doubtless had more on his mind than first-day covers and commemoratives, but that a great man occupied himself with a hobby at a moment of stress is significant. Few of us will ever face the responsibility Mr. Roosevelt faced, but sorting, cataloging, arranging, rearranging, checking, looking at, and just plain enjoying baseball cards can be remarkably satisfying. I get great pleasure from perusing my '56 set, and rearranging the collection.

Leafing through the '56s, I get the effect of gazing at a mandala—what Plato called "the desire and pursuit of the whole." The set is a completed circle, and the more I look at it, the more I find.

What delights can an adult take in baseball cards that a child might not?

There is much in cards that is not obvious. Consider the '56s. The very format of the card invites critical thinking. These horizontal cards have a prominent head shot and an action photo behind. Topps used the same head shots on the '54s, '55s, and '56s. The faces were better pictures than you ever saw on television in those black-and-white days. They were a full-color window to the man's soul. You could see if your idol looked dumb or perverse. The young Hank Aaron looks alert, enthusiastic, and like a man on the verge of greatness.

Then, behind that soul-telling face, was action—an example of that character under pressure.

Owing to the artifice inherent in a hand-tinted card, the '56s contain almost Nabokovian sleights-of-hand. Through use of the airbrush—and what could be more appropriate for the generation that grew up with *Playboy?*—reality has been tinkered with. Aaron is about to slide into home. He looks like a linebacker about to make a tackle. A close examination—not the kind I made then—reveals that the figure beginning his slide is too chunky for Aaron; the markings have been airbrushed off the front of his jersey while a very humble *M* has been added to the cap, and the man, in fact, is none other than Willie Mays. The conflation of those two giants of the fifties and sixties was a commercial expedient, but is also marvelous, inadvertent homage to them both.

The sleight-of-hand on Dave Pope's card is a triumph of fantasy over photography. Pope, a journeyman outfielder whose best years were in the Negro leagues, is making a leaping catch against an outfield wall. Pope was an Oriole in '56, but the action shot is actually a doctored photo from the '54 World Series, when Pope made a gallant but futile effort to catch Dusty Rhodes's tenth-inning, pinch-hit, 260-foot, right-field Polo Grounds home run. That homer was the shortest—most "Chinese," in the parlance of the times—home run in the major leagues, but it won the first game of the biggest upset in Series history since the "Miracle" Braves of 1914 (last place on the Fourth of July: won the World Series) knocked off Connie Mack's

197

"$100,000 infield." On Pope's card, a ball has been airbrushed into his outstretched glove, and World Series history might well be different. It's as if the collective yearnings of the whole city of Cleveland had managed to reshape the past. Such unintended wish-fulfillment is appropriate on a bubble-gum card.

The best action picture on any card is on the '56 Mantle. Mickey is making a one-hand grab by the right-field fence in the old Yankee Stadium. It's one of those pictures you don't forget—a picture that sums up a man's entire career, like Mays's catch off Wertz, or Rose snaring that muffed pop-up in the '80 Series. Mantle looks as if he's jumped straight up in the air and, at the peak of his jump, has pulled a home run out of the bleachers. That card immortalizes one of the great lost features of the old Stadium—the low right-field fence that men would crash into when making spectacular catches, or go over in spectacular fashion pursuing home runs. The most exciting play in baseball is an out-fielder robbing a hitter of a homer. The pitcher has made a mistake, the ball's been hit far enough, and out of the blue—out of the sky, as it were, like divine intervention—an outfielder saves everything by catching the ball over the fence. That is remission of sin.

But why do adults collect?

Anthropologists say objects can be divided into those a culture feels are profane and those that are sacred. Baseball cards, apparently, for some of us, have passed from childish things to sacred items. That American men find spiritual qualities in items intended for children might arouse the ire of Saint Paul, but salvation must be taken where it can. Being a baseball fan is a lifelong occupation with its roots in childhood and its strength in our core selves. The path of baseball's energy takes us to icons that lead to both childhood and eternity, but card collectors are not merely returning to boyhood; they are searching for the self that never changes, the self impervious to time. Baseball cards are pieces of childhood, pieces of deep self, that can be put in an album.

Marcel Proust, the bard of memory, said the only paradise is the paradise we have lost. Perhaps the middle-aged men in T-shirts at card conventions are not so different from Proust's narrator, who spends 7,000 pages tracing a long circle through several levels of society, a generation, and much sexual perversion, back to himself. Those men in T-shirts are looking for that part of themselves which is most real.

At some point in our century—"the American century," as politicians used to call it—sometime after the First World War and certainly by 1925, when F. Scott Fitzgerald published *The Great Gatsby,* the American quest for perfection, salvation, the frontier (call it what you will—it's the search for our best, our freest) started to go backward. America is not only accused of being a nation of adolescents, but a nation that simultaneously rushes into the future while looking backward. This happens at the end of Fitzgerald's novel. Nick Carraway, disgusted by the corruption of the East, thinks back to when he was in prep school, when the world seemed full of mystery and his sensibility was intact. He thinks of girls on the train at Christmastime, then he thinks back all the way to Dutch sailors seeing Long Island for the first time and how beautiful it was (it certainly takes imagination to see Long Island as the "fresh, green breast of the new world"), and this is the vision the book ends with. Not the future, or even Carraway's past, but the deep, imagined past.

At some point, American energy started to backtrack. Where else could it go without a frontier? We believed we were free, and conquered a wild place—but that freedom is gone. Like Jay Gatsby with his ever-receding green light, we are left with a lost childhod, no place to go, and baseball. Baseball is still the national sport, having outlived Indian-killing, kept pace with war, and coexisted with football, and it will survive everything but nostalgia. Perhaps it shouldn't be surprising that baseball's icons have taken root in many adult psyches.

Cards can help us get beyond nostalgia. They stimulate memories that can tell us about ourselves and the game and the country. Baseball cards are icons at the crossroads, icons of the past, present, and imagination. They are Trivia with a capital *T,* not nostalgia. Nostalgia is the soft glow of false memory. Nostalgia is the civics-class version of American history and the Disney version of yourself. It is an American disease. Fitzgerald implies that nostalgia is all that's left of the fresh, green dream—nostalgia and death. And we know what Thomas Wolfe said about going home. American literature, it's been said, is about going home. Nostalgia isn't home. Baseball is an eight-month home. Its history is a place we can always find. Kurt Vonnegut said, "I can't stand living without a culture anymore." No baseball fan ever has to say that. He may have to dig, ask intelligent questions, arrange memorabilia as mandala, but he never has to live without a culture.

Marcel Proust, that strange, elegant, dainty little man who locked himself in a cork-lined room and wrote about the past so extensively that his friends must have wondered if he hadn't found a way to travel in it, wrote eloquently of the taste of the tea-soaked madeleine and how it brought back lost time, said, "And suddenly the memory returns. . . . I ceased to feel mediocre, accidental, mortal." Wouldn't we all? Farther along in that great passage about eating the body and blood of the past, the narrator says, "Seek?" More than that: create." And that is what we all must do with the past—ours and baseball's—seek, indeed, create.

White Suggestions of the Sinister

IN *Gravity's Rainbow,* a novel as complex as a baseball season, Thomas Pynchon says war and baseball are equally given to record-breaking and are both "well-spidered with white suggestions of the sinister." At first this statement seems deliberately obscure or just wrong. Baseball is more like a novel than like a war. It is like an ongoing, hundred-year-old work of art, peopled with thousands of characters, full of improbable events, anecdotes, folklore, and numbers; and futhermore, once the players cross those white, unsinister lines, the game is its own country; who the players are off the field, what they were before and what they will be after, are irrelevant. We resent it when our world—the world of time, money, and death—intrudes, but as Pynchon says, there are suggestions of the sinister.

Despite their immortality in our imaginations, baseball is played by men who sin, suffer, and grow old. Some go to prison, some die violently. The sinister runs like a white thread through the green afternoon.

Only one man has died as a result of injury suffered in a major-league game. The event is famous. Where did it happen and when?

Violent death is antithetical to baseball, but the Antic visits the game. The only major-leaguer fatally injured in a game was Indian shortstop Ray Chapman, who was hit in the head by hard-throwing Carl Mays of the Yankees at the Polo Grounds in 1920. The Indians and Yankees were battling for the pennant, and Chapman, who crowded the plate as much as anyone else in the league, froze when one of Mays's submarine deliveries came at his head. Tris Speaker, who was on deck, said Chapman had time to get out of the way but didn't. He was hit in the temple. Fred Lieb, who witnessed it, said Chapman's left eye was hanging out of its socket. The shortstop took two steps toward first and collapsed. He never regained consciousness and died at three-thirty the next morning, after surgery. Mays, when asked if the pitch was a spitter, said it was "straight as a string." He was exonerated by the police and Commissioner Landis, but vilified by players and fans. Mays blamed the incident for keeping him out of the Hall, but Fred Lieb, who served on the Old Timers' Committee for many years, said suspicions that Mays had dumped a game in the '21 Series, not Chapman's death, kept him out.

Who was the man responsible for making major-leaguers wear batting helmets. When did helmets become mandatory in each league?

Despite Chapman's death, the batting helmet did not become mandatory until 1955 in the National League and 1956 in the American. Branch Rickey decided to make Pirate farmhands wear helmets in the early fifties and lobbied for its use in the major leagues. Rickey helped manufacture some of the first models under the stands at Forbes Field, and no doubt there was "something in it" for the Mahatma. The plastic helmet was designed for Little League use and is the only example of equipment intended for children gaining acceptance in the big leagues.

The dark side of greatness is more associated with artists and writers than with athletes, but a number of players have gone to prison. What decade produced successive MVPs who ran afoul of the law?

The 1960s, that outlaw decade, had two MVPs who did time. Orlando Cepeda, the NL's first unanimous choice in '67, when he led the Cardinals to the pennant and World Series, landed a plane in Puerto Rico full of marijuana, and went to prison in the late seventies. Cepeda admitted his mistake and has regained his status as the island's greatest living ballplayer.

The first man to win the American League MVP and Cy Young Award in the same year is another matter. Denny McLain is a might-have-been of colossal proportions. He won 31 games in '68. Winning 30 games looks more and more like hitting 61 homers as the years go by and no one approaches

207

that figure. When McLain did it, no one had flirted with the pitchers' magic number since 1944, when Hal Newhouser won 29. Nineteen sixty-eight was the year of the pitcher—five men in the American League had ERAs under 2.00, but only four men in the AL and three in the NL won 20 games. Like Maris, McLain did something no one thought possible. Many men have hot starts, and the press ballyhoos a try for 30. (*Time* magazine said Don Drysdale was "Going Like Thirty" in '62. Marichal took a shot at it in '66. Koufax thought he had a chance in '64, but injuries cut his season short.) Everyone loves a statistical barrier, especially one so difficult.

No star ruined his life with quite the dead-end panache of Denny McLain. Stars have ended in the gutter, like Grover Cleveland Alexander, who was an epileptic and an alcoholic and spent his last years as a Bowery bum, and no less than five Cy Young Award winners have had trouble with the law (Dwight Gooden, Vida Blue, Ferguson Jenkins, and Lamar Hoyt had drug-related legal problems—not uncommon for athletes in the 1980s), but Denny McLain was convicted of racketeering.

The first inkling the Tiger right-hander had an eye for the seamy side was an injury suffered at the height of the 1967 pennant race, the wildest in AL history. McLain hurt his foot over the Labor Day weekend. He said he was watching "The Untouchables" on television, his foot went to sleep, and he injured it getting off a couch. Rumor soon had it that McLain was "stomped" by organized crime for not paying gambling debts. In 1970 he was suspended for half the season for associating with gamblers. He was sent to prison in Florida in 1985 on racketeering and drug charges. In 1988 McLain got out and will be tried again, so the sad saga of the first American Leaguer to be MVP and Cy Young Award winner continues.

Name a team of men who died during their playing careers.

This question runs counter to the very idea of baseball—the game is a bulwark against the darkness and a rebellion against time—but it is interesting. Baseball is a place where young men forever run, hit, and throw. It's a place where memory and catechism defeat time in the collective fan imagination, but even into a world so largely imaginary comes death. The game itself is oblivious of time. Roger Angell, in one of his most wonderful pieces, "The Interior Stadium," says, "Since baseball time is measured only in outs, all you have to do is succeed utterly; keep hitting, keep the rally alive, and you have defeated time."

Time, perhaps; death, no.

The pitcher on the dead men's team is Ed Morris, who was stabbed to death at a fish fry in Century, Florida, in 1932, during an argument over a woman. The catcher is Marty Bergen or Willard Hershberger. Bergen, a Boston Beaneaters (they weren't called Braves until 1912) catcher in the last four years of the nineteenth century, and brother of Bill Bergen, who sports one of the lowest lifetime averages in history, killed his wife and two children

209

with an ax, and then cut his throat, in January of 1900. The only player to commit suicide during the season in this century is Willard Hershberger, Ernie Lombardi's backup on the pennant winning '40 Reds. Hershberger played poorly in the second game of a Friday doubleheader in Boston, and cut his throat over the bathtub in his hotel room Saturday afternoon.

The manager is another Boston tragedy. Chick Stahl, a lifetime .307 hitter and playing manager of the Red Sox, killed himself in spring training in 1907. Enough time has passed that one is tempted to make a joke about the quality of the team, or wish other Sox managers had had Stahl's perspicacity, but the way he took his life, swallowing carbolic acid, is such a graphic emblem of a man having his guts eaten out that Stahl's fate is no joke. There were rumors that a "baseball Sadie" (that generation's word for "groupie") was threatening Stahl with exposure, and that, being a family man, he felt vulnerable. Historian Glenn Stout thinks Stahl may have given his new bride venereal disease, and that guilt contributed to his depression, but no one really knows why anyone commits suicide, perhaps not even the suicide. A year later, Stahl's wife was found dead in the doorway of her house in south Boston, possibly the victim of robbery, or of "drugs and alcohol," as the papers put it.

Suicide is both interesting and boring. It is interesting because we all want to know what drives a person over his edge, and boring because, as the relatives of a suicide know, it's the most selfish act a person can commit. The Italian writer Cesare

Pavese said, "No man lacks a good reason for committing suicide," but despite Pavese's wit, no one can really explain the last, fatal moments of suicide.

Self-killing has struck the highest levels of the baseball establishment. National League president Harry Pulliam shot himself during the 1909 season for reasons of ill health and possibly the abuse he suffered for allowing umpire Hank O'Day's decision to stand in the famous Merkle "boner" case. In a game that would have given the New York Giants the 1908 pennant, O'Day called baserunner Fred Merkle out after the winning run had scored in the ninth inning, because Merkle, who had been on first, failed to touch second base when Al Bridwell singled home what looked like the game winner. Merkle, a nineteen-year-old rookie, saw Moose McCormick score, and left the field.

The subsequent rhubarb was the wildest in history. Cub center fielder Solly Hoffman noticed that Merkle hadn't touched second, and threw the ball in, but by this time the crowd was on the field. McGinnity, the Giant first-base coach, seeing what was happening, intercepted the ball. Three Cub players wrestled him for it. A spectator got hold of the ball and was decked by Cub pitcher Rube Kroh, who hadn't been in the game, but who got the ball to Harry Steinfeldt, the third baseman (and answer to the famous question "Who played third with Tinker, Evers, and Chance?"), who got the ball to Tinker, who got it to Evers, who somehow tagged the base in the midst of all this mayhem.

One can see how controversy arose from the play. O'Day ruled in favor of the Cubs and declared the game a tie. NL president Pulliam had the final decision. The Cubs and Giants tied for the season and played a game in the Polo Grounds to make up for the tie. The Cubs won 4 to 2.

That play forever earned Fred Merkle the name "Bonehead," and is the game's most controversial. Pulliam was pilloried and second-guessed. O'Day had been involved in a similar play in Pittsburgh earlier in the month, and had ruled against the Cubs, so he had had the opportunity to think about the legality of failing to touch second after the winning run scores. I suspect O'Day's and Pulliam's decisions were based in part on John McGraw's competitive and irascible personality. Given a chance to beat him on a technicality, they couldn't resist. Pulliam, however, paid dearly for it.

Two of baseball's most famous deaths have been those of first basemen, but they succumbed to illness, not violence. Lou Gehrig's death was ironic in that the disease that bears his name gave Gehrig the immortality that playing in Babe Ruth's shadow had denied him. Harry Agganis, the greatest schoolboy athlete in Massachusetts's history, who had turned a mediocre Boston University football team into a national power and then signed with the Red Sox, died during the '55 season because he played too soon after recovering from pneumonia.

Cubs second baseman Ken Hubbs was Rookie of the Year in 1962. He was one of the few players to field his way to the award, and was also the first Mormon to win it. Hubbs died in a private plane crash in Utah during the winter of '64.

The shortstop on the dead men's team would

be Ray Chapman. I can find no third baseman, but Arky Vaughan died two years after he retired, attempting to save a friend from drowning after a boating accident. Vaughan's early death probably delayed his election to the Hall of Fame, as writers tend to vote for the living.

The most famous outfielder to die during a season is Ed Delahanty. Brooklyn outfielder Len Koenecke suffered the most bizarre death when he went berserk on an airplane he had chartered in 1935. Koenecke was clubbed to death with a fire extinguisher by the pilot as the plane went out of control over a Toronto racetrack. Len was one of those old rookies (twenty-six in '32 when he came up) who used to be more common when there were more minor leagues and baseball was the best job many men could get. Koenecke hit .320 in '34, but Casey Stengel sent Len down in '35, which apparently drove him over the edge.

Baseball deaths are always a shock because baseball is a green world of summer and inner childhood. The players perform on the stage of the game's history, and are surrounded by the illusion of immortality. Lyman Bostock's murder, in 1978, was particularly horrible because it was random. He was shotgunned in Gary, Indiana, while riding in a car with a childhood friend, by her estranged husband, who had decided to kill any man he saw with her. The killer got out of prison in four years.

213

What potential Hall of Famer's career was ruined after a woman was shot in his hotel room?

There is a man who seems to have killed his talent. In December 1973, a woman died of a gunshot in Cesar Cedeno's hotel room in the Dominican Republic, while Cedeno was with her. Cesar said the gun went off by accident, and maybe it did. No charges were filed, but he was never the same. Cedeno and Bobby Bonds were the brightest stars in the National League, the league that had been providing the best players for twenty-five years. Cedeno came up at 19, hit .310, then .264, and .320 twice. He led the NL in doubles his second and third years. He could run, hit, hit with power, even though he played in the Dome, and steal bases like Lou Brock. Whatever happened in that hotel room changed Cedeno's career the way Chappaquiddick changed Ted Kennedy's. Cesar hit .300 once, drove in a hundred runs once, and hit 20 home runs once after the hotel room. He had been expected to do that every year.

Who was the Dodger pitcher that Ernest Hemingway kicked in the balls at Hemingway's hacienda near Havana in 1941?

A number of ex-players have killed themselves, but Hugh Casey's suicide is one of the most interesting because it sheds light on the suicide of a more famous man. Casey was the man Ernest Hemingway kicked below the belt after being outboxed in 1941. Within twenty years both men had shot themselves.

The story of Hemingway and Casey's boxing match ("grace under pressure," my ass—"kick you in the balls" is more like it) was told by Billy Herman, the Dodger second baseman, in Donald Honig's excellent book, *Baseball When the Grass Was Real.* The scene was better than a novel: the world-famous writer glad-handed some Brooklyn Dodgers, who were in spring training in Havana, into coming out to his hacienda for drinks—Papa presumably wanted to drink whiskey with real men, and talk real talk in those famous sentences—and the scene developed into something worthy of the theater of the absurd.

After more than a few drinks, Papa decided to get out the gloves. One has to admire Hemingway's fascination with boxing. He wasn't good at it. Morley Callaghan, who was five-seven, beat Hemingway, who was six-two, quite badly in a match Scott Fitzgerald let go on too long in Paris in 1929; but Callaghan could box, and Hemingway, like most of us, was merely an aficionado. Boxing was a way for him to touch men and receive punishment at the same time.

Casey was the only ballplayer who wanted to fight. After a few rounds, Hemingway was getting the worst of it, so he kicked Casey in the balls. The pitcher got up, whacked the bejesus out of the old poseur, declined an invitation to stay and fight a duel, and returned to the Dodger camp. The next day, with a hangover and the hangdog charm Hemingway was so capable of, the writer was led back to the Dodger camp by his wife, and apologized.

Herman's story ends in Havana, but that wasn't

the end of Casey and Hemingway. They became friends. Whatever boxing, ball-kicking, humiliation, and braggadocio were a substitute for, both men needed it. They saw each other in the States. Kirby Higbe tells of hearing Casey talking pitching, and Hemingway watching in rapt admiration; or of Hemingway talking writing, and Casey taking it all in with wonderment. Sometimes the relationship was less platonic, and they'd rent a hotel room and beat the hell out of each other.

Two years after Casey retired, beset with financial and marital difficulties, he shot himself in the head with a rifle he fired with his toe. Hemingway said the pitcher had "done it like a man." The author and would-be boxer blew his own brains out ten years later.

Boston and New York Questions

THERE'S nothing like a rivalry, and New York and Boston have a hot one. The 1986 World Series added a new twist as the Red Sox found another New York team they couldn't beat. At first glance, the Boston–New York affair may seem provincial and one-sided, since the Red Sox almost never beat the Yankees when it counts, but this conflict is deeper than the standings. It goes to the heart of being a fan.

Does everyone have a predisposition to the Red Sox or the Yankees?

The Red Sox and the Yankees are as different as Athens and Sparta. A person either likes underdogs, long odds, and lost causes, or identifies with power and privilege. Another way of saying this is that life is a comedy for Yankee fans, and a tragedy for Red Sox fans. The Yankees, in a very real sense, are New York. They have the biggest market area, a huge stadium, and economic clout. The Red Sox are Boston: comfortable, neurotic, self-conscious. The Yankees are winners. The Red Sox are stylish losers.

Not woeful losers, but last-minute, star-crossed, drive-you-out-of-your-mind losers. They are talented, self-destructive, attractive.

Is it possible for a team to commit an original sin?

Until 1920, the Red Sox had been in five World Series and won them all. Then they sold Babe Ruth to New York. They have been in four Series, and lost them all. The Yankees had never won a pennant until they got Ruth. They have won 33 subsequently. Is Boston really laboring under a curse? If not, how can the '86 World Series be explained?

In '86, Boston came within one strike of beating the Mets. Who was the man Calvin Schiraldi had one swing from oblivion, but who hung in for a single?

The answer is Gary Carter—a player as disliked as anyone in baseball, but a tough out. Do you remember who got the next hit? I actually thought the Red Sox were going to win, and triumph over New York, as they did in 1912. A rational man doesn't believe a team can commit an Unforgivable Sin.

I, like many lifelong Sox fans, waited for what should have been the last out, and wondered what I'd do if they won. I thought I'd have to change my philosophy of life. The world wouldn't be the same. I have always known the Red Sox to lose big games, and I am fated to root for them. This is the unavoidable order of things. As Schiraldi wound up, I thought: Maybe there is a God? Maybe the universe is benign; maybe there is justice besides poetic justice. But I also knew that if they won, they'd be just another team rather than an infuriating emblem of my psyche. For a moment I was ambivalent. If the Red Sox won, part of me would change, but don't think I didn't want them to win. I'd have gladly traded my sense of the universe for the World Championship. I just didn't know what I'd do. Weep? Repent? Vote Republican?

Kevin Mitchell got a hit.

I thought of the curse, but patterns can be broken. People change, don't they?

Ray Knight singled. Carter scored.

I was like a child watching a horror movie. I didn't want to look, but I did.

Who came in to pitch for Boston?

Bob Stanley, the Red Sox's overweight, over-the-hill, million-dollar ex-stopper. Schiraldi had become the stopper in August, and, after Roger Clemens, had been the most important man on the team. The old stopper replaced the new stopper, and I wanted to cover my eyes. There was no reason to assume Stanley could do what Schiraldi hadn't, but I kept hoping. Once Stanley threw a mean spitter, now he throws a mean change-up.

Who was up?

Mookie Wilson, and I prayed he'd be a Red Sox for just one at-bat. Stanley got two strikes on him, but as it had proved for Schiraldi, two strikes was the dead man's hand. Stanley tried to cross him up with an inside pitch. He threw low and inside, and Wilson jackknifed. The ball went to the backstop. Mitchell scored and the game was tied. The philosopher Nietzsche said, "Die at the right time," but I think he meant something else.

The pitch was bad, but Gedman should have knocked it down. Carter knocked down three or four worse than that, but, obnoxious as he is, Carter is a money ballplayer. Gedman is a Red Sox.

I knew all was lost. It didn't matter if the Sox got out of the inning. They were a corpse after the wild pitch. For some teams a wild pitch would be shooting themselves in the foot, for Boston it's a bullet in the head. Wilson hit a grounder to first and it went through Bill Buckner's legs. The game, and the Series, as Dwight Evans said later, was over. What infuriated me was that Buckner didn't even chase the ball.

Has there ever been a bigger Series goat than Bill Buckner?

Never. Buckner not only let that ball get through his legs, but intimidated Red Sox manager John McNamara (not a difficult task) into letting him stay in the game, even though he had been replaced by the better-fielding Stapleton in the other Sox victories. Buckner killed the Sox with his hitting. He stranded 27 men and finished something like 17 innings, which helped Jim Rice drive in no-runs in seven games. Buckner was hurt. He couldn't dig in or

222

drive off his back foot when batting, but McNamara played him, and played him, and played him. It was like Don Zimmer and Butch Hobson in '78.

Is winning the LCS in miraculous fashion enough to redeem the World Series?

Unfortunately not, and this is the result of yearly playoffs. Bobby Thompson's home run is the most dramatic event in baseball history because it capped a great pennant race and won an unscheduled playoff. The amazing turnaround in game five of the '86 LCS—when the Red Sox, like the Mets, were within a strike of elimination, but came back on a Don Baylor two-run homer, a hit batsman, and Dave Henderson's two-out, two-strike, ninth-inning homer—was wonderful, but the way Boston lost the Series obscures the LCS victory. Had the Mets beaten the Sox in five or six games, as they should have, Boston fans would remember only the Henderson homer.

What's more painful, losing the Series or blowing the regular season?

Bad as the '86 Series was, Boston's '78 collapse was worse. In '78 the Sox led the Yankees by 14½ games on July 18, by 9 on August 13, and by 6 and a half on September 1, lost 14 out of 17, should have been out of it, climbed back, were tied on the last day of the season, and lost a one-game playoff. It was the quintessential Red Sox year.

There's no experience like watching a team lose

a lead late in the season. Losing the World Series is merciful by comparison. August and September don't end after four games. A late-season disintegration is the death of a thousand cuts. Losing the Series is suicide, but losing the season is eternal damnation. It's a lost year—all those early wins, all that good pitching, all those rallies, all that luck, all the little things done right; insurance players picked up, the overachieving of mediocre players, career years by good players, and great play by great players—but worse, all the years spent waiting, all the empty Septembers, dreary winters, and hopeful Aprils, go unatoned.

There is no four-game buy-out. The '78 season didn't end after the Boston Massacre. The Yankees came into Fenway Park in September four games out and swept the Red Sox by outscoring them 42 to 9, but the season didn't stop. (The scores were 15–3, 13–2, 7–0, and 7–4, which sound like football scores.) Humiliation led to more humiliation.

Watching a lead disappear is excruciating. You lose and lose and lose and nothing stops it. Every flaw and weakness returns to kill you. Fear breeds losing, and losing breeds fear. Losing encourages *them*. *They* win and you lose. *They* come from behind and you can't hold a lead. *They* move runners, steal bases, capitalize on errors. You are paralyzed. All your faults are revealed. Your strengths are not only false. They're gone.

It had to be the Yankees. It had to be the store-bought, late-seventies Yankees, that extension of George Steinbrenner's checkbook and ego, that squealing imitation of the great Yankees: Reggie instead of Mickey, Thurman Munson instead of Berra, Graig Nettles instead of Roger Maris. Marx said great events happen twice, the first time as tragedy, the second as farce, but this farce had Ron Guidry, who established the season-winning percentage mark for a starting pitcher by going 25–3.

I know how they felt in Brooklyn in '42, in Brooklyn in '51, in Philly in '64. I saw a hard-won season go down the drain, and it felt like my life went with it. The '78 Red Sox were like the French Army in 1940, on their backs as quickly as a Parisian whore. The first crack in the armor came before the All-Star Game, when Rick Burleson hurt his ankle stealing a base. Boston supposedly had a super sub, Frank Duffy. (What a monument to futility his career was: the Giants gave up George Foster to get him, and gave him up with Gaylord Perry to get Sam McDowell). Duffy was horrible, which foreshadowed the collapse of the infield under the doomed leadership of Butch Hobson. Hobson had bone chips in his elbow. The club knew this in the spring, but didn't want to operate because it might affect the team's start. They were right. Hobson's play didn't affect the club's start, it merely destroyed the season.

Hobson couldn't make routine throws. His errors were infectious. The infield quickly brought down the pitching staff. Only Dennis Eckersley was any good. Tiant couldn't win, Lee lost six in a row, Torrez won one out of ten, Drago was abysmal, Campbell had been burned out by Zimmer the year before. A rookie named Bobby Sprowl started against the Yankees because Zimmer hated Bill Lee. Sprowl got bombed. It was a nightmare.

No team's collapse was ever so rooted in character. All the bigotry and foolishness of the organization was epitomized by Don Zimmer, who even looked like a fool. Zimmer resembled the sergeant on "Hogan's Heroes," and was as easy to outwit. Don didn't like players who'd been to college, he didn't like criticism, he didn't like talk shows, he didn't like people who were smarter than he was. Zimmer was a 1970s manager with a 1910 brain.

Nineteen seventy-eight was a tragedy of character. Zimmer managed as if he were trying to make a point. He preferred to lose with men who had the "right stuff," like an over-the-hill Bob Bailey or a crippled Butch Hobson, than win with better players. Boston fans had to watch a major-league manager who believed that how you played the game was more important than winning.

The Red Sox staged a late-September comeback. It started when Hobson finally asked to be taken out of the lineup and was replaced with Jack Brohamer. Hobson was enough of a competitor to take to the bench himself. Unlike Bill Buckner in the '86 Series, Hobson was finally willing to sacrifice his ego. Butch sat, the team won, the race got interesting, and the Red Sox went to their destiny.

That destiny, as the '86 World Series proved, is to get as close as possible before losing. There is a demonic perfection in the way the Red Sox torment their fans. They came back in '78 just enough to make losing really sting. They took three out of four from Detroit and swept Toronto, Rick Waits defeated the Yankees on the last day of the season as Tiant beat the Blue Jays (his last Boston win), and then there was the playoff.

It wasn't the greatest game ever played. If the Red Sox had won, it might have been because they would have been beating history, Harry Frazee, the Curse, and Original Sin; but they didn't. They got an early lead, just like the last games of the '75 and '86 World Series, and lost. There were some great moments. Yaz homered off Guidry in the first—an old man guessing fastball against a pitcher who had the greatest season I've ever seen. Yaz's drive hit the foul pole. That homer was grit. Yaz just had to do something in a game that big. Bucky Dent's homer, which made the score 3–2 New York in the seventh, is supposed to be the nadir of being a Sox fan. I disagree. Home runs frequently get popped into the screen by unlikely sluggers. Freddy Patek once hit 3 in a game in Fenway. What infuriated me was Reggie Jackson's eighth-inning homer off Stanley. I'll never forget a friend of mine screaming, "Don't pitch to him! This is his spot!" And then the ball was in the center-field bleachers. That made it 5–2, and of course, the Sox lost 5–4.

It was a great game, and Tom Boswell described it beautifully in *How Life Imitates the World Series,* but the outcome was so predictable, it wasn't the greatest ever.

Was '78 the worst choke in history?

No, the Phillies' collapse in '64 was worse because the Phillies did not recover and force a playoff. The Phillies, who had played over their heads all summer, had a six-and-a-half-game lead with eleven to play, and lost. The end started when Chico Ruiz, a Cincinnati imp of the perverse, stole home, and hell followed. Mauch overmanaged. He kept pitching Bunning and Short, and lost. Mauch established a pattern for himself. He managed longer than any man without winning a pennant. Mauch got close in '82, with a 2–0 lead on the Brewers in the LCS; and he, like the Red Sox, got within one strike in '86.

It's ridiculous, isn't it, to believe in curses, omens, and jinxes, and to think the weight of the past rests on the living like the Pharoahs' curse, but how does one explain Gene Mauch, the post-Ruth Red Sox, or the losses the Brooklyn Dodgers suffered at the hands of the Yankees? We live in a Bill James age of analysis, in which our prejudices, intuitions, and memories are rigorously discredited with cold, hard numbers, but how can one explain the Boston Red Sox without sounding like William Butler Yeats on the subject of gyres? Is it possible that curses, archetypes, and Fate operate in this age of software and James? Can a team be cursed? Are there questions beyond numbers? Religion explains the unexplainable. Art makes it bearable. Who can explain the Red Sox?

On the last day of what season did the Red Sox not only lose the pennant in New York, but see Ted Williams lose an unprecedented third Triple Crown?

Nineteen forty-nine. The late-forties Red Sox were cursed. They lost the '46 Series in seven games, on Slaughter's slide (they had been favored; Sox slugging and pitching seemed to outweigh NL left-handed guile and speed). In '48 they lost the first one-game playoff to a knuckleballing rookie named Gene Beardon, who never had a winning season again, and to home runs by Ken Keltner and Lou Boudreau. (I hope there's a place in hell for the inventor of the Williams shift; Boudreau grossly took advantage of Williams's character. Of course, Ted fought it instead of hitting to left. Ted fought everything, even enemies of the United States. He never did anything the easy way.) The Red Sox, who also don't do anything the easy way, started thirty-six-year-old Denny Galehouse. This may be the worst choice of a starting pitcher in the history of baseball. Galehouse was 8–7 and would pitch only two more innings in the major leagues. Why did he have to pitch the playoff game against the Indians?

Parnell and Kinder said they could have pitched. Joe McCarthy, who managed the Cubs and Yankees brilliantly, but whose brain became Zimmer in Boston, said no one told him anything. Being a Red Sox manager, he didn't ask. Like Darrell Johnson using Jim Burton (Burton was a rookie!!! He had 53 innings of major-league experience!!!) in the ninth inning of the seventh game of the '75 World Series, McCarthy picked his worst pitcher and used him in the biggest situation of his life.

The '49 tragedy is deeper than stupidity. Character was fate. Ted Williams lived out his archetype and fulfilled his flawed perfectionist destiny. Not only did the Red Sox lose the pennant on the last day of the season in New York—they went to the Bronx with a one-game lead and two to play—but Williams lost a third Triple Crown. This is the larger tragedy. The Red Sox have lost many pennants, but a chance for three Triple Crowns doesn't happen even once a generation.

The Triple Crown is rare. Who was the last National Leaguer to win it?

It hasn't been done in the NL since Joe Medwick in 1937. Had Williams won three, he would have been known forever as the Triple Crown King. It would have been like 56 straight or Peter Rose's amazing collection of hits: one of a kind.

On September 20, 1949, Ted Williams led in all three categories: .350, 40 HRs, and 153 RBIs. These figures would have made lordly season totals, but there were two weeks to go. On September 20, the Red Sox were three games behind the Yankees. George Kell was hitting .341. Williams's teammate Vern Stephens, who Ted credited with getting him fastballs near the plate, had 39 homers and 150 RBIs. The '49 Red Sox, needless to say, were the last team to have two men with 150 RBIs, and Williams was the last man to score a 150 and drive in a 150 in the same season.

Ted was always accused of not hitting in the clutch. This is a difficult charge to refute, because no one hits in the clutch all the time. If a man plays on a Series winner, the question becomes moot; if not, like allegations against his masculinity, it lingers. A Boston writer, one of that tribe of backbiting, inbred hacks who were as lethal and internecine as the Jesuits, wrote that Williams hit .200 in the ten biggest games of his life. That story so typifies Boston writers of the period that I've seen it attributed by Peter Gammons to Dave Egan, and by John Updike in his magnificent piece "Hub Fans Bid Kid Adieu" to Huck Finnigan. The Updike article, as befits Williams, is the best baseball piece I've ever read, and that includes Angell. Updike covered Ted's last game for *The New Yorker,* and wrote that superbly compressed, wonderfully literate story, which is the first baseball writing I ever read that was great writing. Roger Angell's myriad voice may well have been licensed by Updike's single piece. Updike was twenty-eight at the time, and readers seeing the story must have thought they were seeing something like the young Ted Williams, but Updike's career has been more like Lou Brock's— good, but no Triple Crown.

In '49, Williams went right at Destiny. This wasn't a blown lead. Boston looked out of it early. The Red Sox started the season by losing to the Yankees on Opening Day. They had one of those commanding but illusory Fenway leads, and McCarthy took Williams out. New York came back and

beat the Splinterless Sox. In June, the Yankees
came in for three, and Joe DiMaggio wasn't supposed to play. Joe was hobbled by injuries the whole
season, but recovered enough to hit four home runs
in the three games, and New York swept. '49 illus-
trates the difference between Williams and Di-
Maggio, between New York and Boston. Joe could
play only 76 games, be hurt all year, and come
down with pneumonia, but he hit when it mattered,
and his team won. Williams's achievements are statistical and mythic. The pressure he thrived on was
the pressure of numbers. Ted's game was perfection. Joe's was baseball. No one could say Joe Di-
Maggio hit .200 in the ten biggest games of his life.

Despite the bad start, the Red Sox, as always,
didn't go quietly. They couldn't fall apart and allow
Williams to concentrate on his stats and achieve
immortality with a third Triple Crown. The team is
too interesting and perverse. They were eleven and
a half out in August, and started to win. They came
at New York the way New York came at them in '78.
For almost two months Boston was the unblinking,
predatory comer. With eight games left, they were
two out. Five of those eight were with New York.

The first two were in Fenway, and Boston won
both, beating Lopat and Reynolds. Williams always
said Lopat, a crafty left-hander, gave him trouble,
but in that game, Ted homered off Lopat for the
first time; and Ellis Kinder shut out the Yankees 3–
0. The next day the Red Sox won 4–1 behind Mel
Parnell, and Williams hit his forty-third homer.

They went to New York on Monday, for a
makeup game, and the Red Sox reached the pinna-

cle of their season. In the second inning, Sox outfielder Al Zarilla made one of those old Yankee
Stadium right-field, in-the-stands catches to rob
Johnny Lindell of a home run. The catch made *Life*
magazine. Boston trailed 6–3 in the eighth, and in
most un–Red Sox–like fashion, scored four times.
The big play was a safe call at home, which so infuriated Yankee third-string catcher and later Red
Sox manager Ralph Houk, that he started a brawl
for which he, Casey Stengel, and Cliff Mapes were
fined.

Boston was in first place by one. They had won
ten in a row. Williams was hitting .349, Kell .343.
Arthur Daley wrote in the *Times,* "No longer can
the Yankees win the pennant. The Red Sox have to
lose it." These are, I believe, the truest words ever
spoken.

Boston beat Washington and the Yankees beat
the Athletics on Tuesday. On Wednesday, as fate
would have it, New York beat Philadelphia and the
Senators beat Boston 2–1 on a ninth-inning wild
pitch by Mel Parnell, the Red Sox's best pitcher.

It rained on the East Coast on Thursday, and
neither New York nor Boston played. They both
played Friday and won. The Red Sox got 18 hits and
14 walks against the Senators, but Williams went 0
for 3, just as he had in the 2–1 loss. The next day
they went to "shoot it out in the Bronx," as the
Times so vividly put it. Boston was ahead by one,
with two to play.

The games were Red Sox to the bone. Boston
had a 4–0 lead on Saturday and blew it, losing 5 to
4 on an eighth-inning home run by Johnny Lindell.

Boston got only four hits, and one was by Williams. In the second, with Pesky on first, Ted hit a line drive that should have been a double, but Fate, Curse, Character, and Red Sox luck intervened. The ball hit umpire Cal Hubbard, a former football player and a behemoth of a man, and fell at Hubbard's feet for a single. Pesky stayed at second. The line drive couldn't, of course, hit Hubbard and bounce toward the stands, or just miss him, the way line drives usually do. The Red Sox just don't have pennant luck. In the '78 playoff, Lou Pinella played out of position on Fred Lynn's liner in the sixth and what should have been a two-run double was an out. In the eighth, blinded by the sun, Pinella somehow got his glove on Jerry Remy's base hit and kept Burleson from going to third, where he could have scored on Rice's fly. Burleson, and the hopes of all decent men, died on third. How did Pinella do those things? It's luck. It's fate. It's Boston.

Pesky stayed on second. Williams had to hold on first. When the Red Sox did score, they got one run instead of two. They lost the game, of course, by one run. Williams was hitting .344, Kell .341.

The Sunday game, like the last game of the '75 World Series and the sixth game of the '86 Series, was a manager's folly. New York led 1–0 in the top of the eighth. Kinder and Vic Raschi were locked in a pennant-deciding duel. Joe McCarthy decided it was time for the old Boston idiocy. He pinch-hit for Kinder—just like Johnson hitting for Willoughby in '75. Why do Red Sox managers always invoke "the book" in situations where every cogent being in the universe knows they shouldn't?

234

A rookie up from Louisville, Tom Wright, hit for Kinder, and walked. Dom DiMaggio hit into a double play. A tired Parnell and Tex Hughson came on to give up four runs, 5–0 Gotham. The big hit was a pop fly by Jerry Coleman that Al Zarilla couldn't catch, which fell for a bases-clearing double. That moment is the epitome of post-Ruth Red Sox history. Zarilla, a good-hitting outfielder but average runner, came in as hard as he could, dove for the pop fly, and missed it. For me, this moment is frozen, like the scene on Keats's urn, where the fair youth, who will never grow old, is reaching for the maiden, who cannot fade. ("Bold lover, never canst thou kiss. . . ." Never wilt thou catch that pop fly. . . .) The moment is a frozen emblem of Red Sox futility, and Zarilla will never get there. His frustration, and ours, is his immortality.

In the ninth, the Red Sox rallied. They didn't tie, of course, but they scored three and had the tying run at the plate when Birdie Tebbits popped up to first baseman Henrich to end the game. Two runs scored when a hobbled DiMaggio couldn't get to a long Bobby Doerr fly. Joe took himself out of the game. Can you imagine a Boston player doing that?

Williams went 0 for 2 in the last game. Kell went 2 for 3 in his last game. The final averages were Kell .3429, Williams .34275. Ted lost everything.

What is the greatest individual performance that led a team to the pennant?

This honor belongs to a Red Sox, not a Yankee. Rooting for Boston has not always been a trail of tears. There is one year, one September, and one player who, during that burst of pot, rock, and sexuality known as the Summer of Love, redeems the whole melancholy adventure of rooting for the Boston Red Sox. The man was Carl Yastrzemski, and he is a representative figure of the late sixties, when all hell broke loose, and for a brief moment underdogs, minorities, and notions like brotherhood and revolution captured the popular imagination. Carl Yastrzemski hit .522 in the last two weeks of 1967, as he powered a team that had come in ninth the year before to a pennant. Every game counted. Boston did not get into first until the last day of the season. Yaz got 23 hits in 44 at-bats. He had five homers and 16 RBIs.

The Red Sox played the Twins on the final two days of the 1967 season. They were a game behind Minnesota and a game in front of Detroit, who, because of rain-outs, had to play two doubleheaders on those same two days. It was the end of the wildest AL race since 1908, and by Jesus, the Red Sox, with a mediocre team, a great manager, a twenty-game winner, Carl Yastrzemski, and the grace of God, won the pennant. Yaz, like Williams in '49, was battling for the Triple Crown. He went 7 for 8 in the two games, hit a home run, as Killebrew did, to tie for the homer lead, had five RBIs, made a great throw to end a Twins rally, and Boston finally won under pressure. The story of that race, and Boston's otherworldly finish, is brilliantly recounted in Roger Angell's "The Flowering and Deflowering of New England," a piece that lives up to its title. Red Sox fans cling to that summer. It's like having seen Jesus, the rest of history is bearable. Darrell Johnson can't bring in a rookie to lose the last game against the Twins. Don Zimmer can't ruin the season with stupidity. Haywood Sullivan can't lose it to free-agency. John McNamara can't let Bill Buckner blow it. No one can ruin 1967—not even the Yankees.

Epilogue

BASEBALL has changed me.

How much of my spirit was shaped that night when I saw Yankee Stadium and Ted Williams? How much of my sense of wonder crystallized that chilly evening with the stride of the great hitter?

How many times, down the years, when alone, have I turned to the *Encyclopedia* and the Fireside books and Angell and old sports' sections and SABR's publications, and the game's long history . . .

I listen late at night. My wife is asleep. My son moves in his crib as if the Red Sox are troubling his sleep. Millions of people are listening to baseball.

The night belongs to us.

Acknowledgments

L IKE most enterprises, this book did not spring full-blown from the author's head. I would like to acknowledge the following: the Society for American Baseball Research, for providing a network and an atmosphere where fans can meet and exchange ideas and information; Bob Gurland, my baseball mentor; Bill Brevda, for a lifetime of friendship; Paul Adomites, fellow traveler on my baseball odyssey; David Brandt, great friend and great fan; Cappy Gagnon, for friendship and encouragement; Dick Johnson, for ideas and friendship; Glenn Stout, poet and historian; SABR members who sent trivia questions even though they weren't used; Ed Rubin for wit and wisdom; Pete Palmer, the most accessible expert I have ever met; Rich Tourangeau, creator of the Play Ball calendars; Bill Haber, the great biographical researcher; Bill James, for helpful comments; Andy, Dave, and Joe, the guys at Bay State Coin; Scott Flatow, Trivia genius; Casey Ichnaiowski, for telling me about Babe Ruth's record against the Yankees; Mike Fahey for friendship and humor; Jake Shearer, whose wit I have been plagiarizing for twenty years; Mason Salisbury, for ideas, encouragement, and a lifetime of baseball conversation; the Boston University Creative Writing Program and Leslie Epstein, whose intelligence and intolerance of mediocrity is an inspiration; Hugh O'Neill, for suggesting, editing, and guiding this project; and my wife, Barbara, for everything.

About the Author

LUCIUS ALBERT SALISBURY III was born on April 12, 1947, in Rhinebeck, New York, but now lives in Boston, where he teaches English at Bunker Hill Community College. He has been a member of the Society for American Baseball Research since 1979 and vice president since 1987. He is married and has one son, Lucius Albert Salisbury IV, known as "Ace."